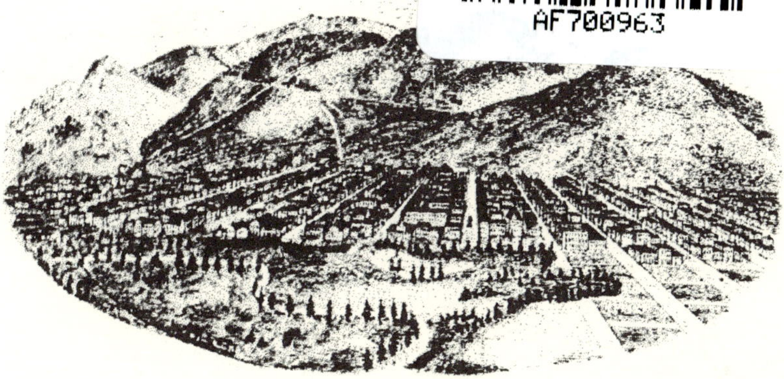

ASPEN.

THE BATTLE OVER SILVER:

PORTER NELSON IN ASPEN

by

Robert B. Houston, Jr.

"You shall not crucify mankind on a cross of gold!"

William Jennings Bryan, 1896

THE BATTLE OVER SILVER: PORTER NELSON IN ASPEN

TABLE OF CONTENTS

PREFACE

Like so many, I began, late in life, to research my roots. I learned that at age 24, my Nelson grandfather had given up considerable comfort in Culpeper, Virginia to go West. First he worked for the Santa Fe Railroad. After returning for a short stay in Virginia, he moved to Aspen, Colorado to become a trader in mining properties. Mining and the West were completely new to the Virginia boy.

Nelson's venturing, at the tender age of 24, into a life completely new to him intrigued me; I saw similarities between his life and mine. I too had moved into a world foreign to me. At age 22, I left a career in physics to join the US Foreign Service. When Nelson became a trader in mining properties, he began a career for which he had little or no formal training. When I took up the life of a diplomat, I too began a career for which I lacked formal schooling. Porter Nelson made his move in the mid-1880's, shortly after the West was freed of any serious Indian menace and was widely accessible by rail. I made my move at the end of World War II, when much of the world was freed of the Axis menace and open again to American diplomacy.

But there were differences between Porter Nelson's moves and mine. Nelson had just taken on responsibility for a wife when he began his new career in mining; in his new life, he was risking his inheritance. When I became a Foreign Service Officer, earning a steady salary, responsible only for myself, I was taking no such gamble. I had to admire Nelson's chutzpa; he showed more daring than I had. I came to feel that I <u>had</u> to recount his life story. By so doing, I thought I might find answers to two big questions: why did he give up an easy life in Virginia to go West? Why did he stay on in Colorado so long after things went sour?

In 1888, when Porter Nelson settled there, Aspen was the world's most active silver mining center. Here Porter Nelson willy-nilly became a pawn in the battle over silver's role in the nation's monetary system, a battle that went on for over two decades. I saw this battle as a fascinating and educational story, worth recording for its own sake, but tightly woven in with Porter Nelson's life. Thus I would write a book with three basic topics: Nelson, silver, Aspen.

Now, the how of the book. When I decided to write Porter Nelson's life story, I ruled out two things. I would not write an academic book with copious foot notes; Nelson's life is not important history, but a human interest story. I would not write a book analyzing the events of the 1880-1946 period, using hindsight to appear wiser than the folk who lived through the events. I would do this so that the reader, confronted with the same dilemmas and choices as did those involved with silver in the latter years of the 19th century, would come to his own conclusions, not just read mine.

In keeping with these principles, I recount the events in the present tense, as I believe they were perceived by persons alive at the time. The contemporary press is my source of information on the important events of the period. Two Aspen newspapers, the weekly Rocky Mountain Sun, and the Aspen Democrat, are my primary sources for information on the doings of Porter Nelson and on Aspen happenings. The Sun and the Democrat supported the Populists and later the Democrats. For periods when the these two papers are not available, I use the pro-Republican Aspen Daily Times. No surprise: all Aspen papers were pro-silver. For a national and international perspective, I use the generally anti-silver New

York Times. Along with the contemporary press, I of course draw upon available and relevant family material, including photographs. None of this material has been researched before.

I realize that my organizational scheme may cause my story to seem disorganized; well, that's life. I realize too that in the mid-1990's, it is impossible for me to dig out the full range of events that Porter Nelson and others of his time dealt with. But I have to try, so as to answer as best I can the big questions still puzzling me about my grandfather's life.

I frequently recount Aspen newspaper reports on the comings and goings of various residents (especially Porter Nelson). Aspen papers of the time were very nosy about the activities of the locals; probably this helped sell papers. The reader should not think that I believe these happenings are of great importance; they're not. My hope in repeating these tidbits is that I'm making a contribution, such as it is, to knowledge of Aspen social history in the period 1890-1910.

The reader should not conclude from the title of my book that the Nelson family could not see beyond Aspen and silver mining. Porter looked elsewhere (even into gold in Nevada). His wife invested in gold mines away from Aspen, as well as in farms and irrigation systems in Delta County, Colorado. Like many Aspenites, Porter Nelson was particularly attracted to the complex ores of Crystal in Gunnison County. But I keep Aspen and silver as the major foci of the book.

I must acknowledge that I was fortunate to receive generous help in writing this book. Special thanks go to Mrs. Mary Ellen Shoemaker in Basalt, to Ms. Jennifer Bosley of the Colorado Historical Society in Denver, and Linda Miller of Roanoke College in Salem, Virginia, for help in gathering material. I owe a particular debt to cousins who provided valuable family material. Marguerite Noetzli generously gave me photographs her mother had saved from the Aspen period. Porter and Jim Nelson kindly made available photographs and documentary material of a family nature; these gave me valuable new insights into my grandfather's life.

Larry Fredrick of Aspen read an early version of the chapters on Aspen, and pointed out several errors in my understanding of Aspen events. Jim Nelson reviewed portions of my draft and made helpful suggestions. Professor Duane Vandenbushe of Western State College took time from a busy schedule to comment on my Crystal chapter. My book would be poorer without these contributions. But I alone am responsible for the selection of material used, and for errors of interpretation of this material.

Last but not least, I must bow toward my wife, Suzy, whose patience I sorely tested by the frequent "time outs" from normal household tasks I took in writing this book. She went with me to courthouses for research. She "deciphered" my grandmother's letters to her husband, written in a most unusual script. Suzy also allowed her arm to be twisted into proofreading much of my draft. I am fortunate to have had such a helpmate, not just for 33 years like my grandfather Nelson, or not just for 14 years like my own father. Thanks, my dear, for putting up with my many foibles for going on half a century.

Arlington, Virginia, November, 1996

CHAPTER ONE

METAL IN THE MONEY

Well-meaning friends tell me I should bury the tough stuff, like the metal content of money, in a footnote in the middle of the book. Best to start my book with a catchy sentence or two: "The old man took his last breath just as the old grandfather clock in the gloomy hall tolled midnight." I give my friends all the respect they deserve, but I am not writing a novel where such a slick literary trick might be appropriate. No! This is a straightforward book, chock full of facts. I will dish out the meat up front, beginning with the origins of the current US monetary system.

The founding fathers, in their wisdom, provide in Section 8, paras. 5 and 6 of the Constitution that the new Federal Government shall have the power to "regulate" the nation's money, whatever that means. Because monarchs often cheated their people by "debasing" the precious metal content of a nation's coins,[1] the Founding Fathers give the Congress, not the President,[2] the power to "regulate" the money.

---

1. Congress early on shows its strong abhorrence of debasing of coins. The 1792 law setting up the first US mint provides that any mint employee who, for purpose of private gain, turns out debased coins "shall be deemed guilty of felony and shall suffer death."
2. In 1933, Congress delegates to the President (Franklin D. Roosevelt) limited authority to change the metal content of the nation's coinage. Roosevelt uses this power in 1934.

To exercise its power to "regulate" coinage, Congress in April, 1792 enacts a Mint Act (1 Stat. 246) setting up a mint and naming seven coins for the new nation. The unit of account is called the dollar, patterned after the Spanish milled dollar then in common use in the states. The Act describes three gold coins, four silver coins, and two copper coins. The gold coins are the Eagle worth $10, the Half Eagle worth $5, and the Quarter Eagle worth $2.50. The four silver coins are the dollar, the quarter dollar, the disme (sic) and the half disme. The two copper coins are the cent and the half cent. The law says the US monetary system is bi-metallic, with coins of the "precious" metals gold and silver both being legal tender. The coins are of varying degrees of purity, but law defines the ratio of the two metals in pure state as 15:1.

On January 18, 1837, another Mint Act (5 Stat. 136) provides a uniform .900 fineness for gold and silver coins, and cuts the gold content of the $10 Eagle from 247.5 grains set in 1792 to 232.2 grains. This makes the legal silver-to-gold ratio 16:1, a ratio silver miners later consider written in stone.[3] Remember: "bi-metallic," "bi-metallism," and "16:1".

The mint laws imply ceiling prices for the various metals. For example: the 1792 law saying that 347 1/4 grains of pure silver equals $1 in effect assumes that the silver price will always be below $1.29 an ounce. Likewise, the law of 1837 setting 232.2 grains of gold equal to $10 in effect assumes a market price of gold less than $20.67 an ounce. If either metal were to go above these limits, no citizen

---

3. Well, the ratio of 371 1/4 to 23.22 is not exactly 16:1, but close enough for government work. The Mint Act of 1834 (4 Stat. 774) had already devalued silver from the 15:1 ratio.

will present bullion for coinage. Further, the public will melt down or export the affected coins. Heaven forbid that.

The cost of the bullion needed to make a silver dollar varies over time; in the 1890's, that cost is well below 50 cents. At that price, the profit in coining a silver dollar is 100%. Recall the expression "coining money?" Coinage profit is called "seignorage" and normally goes to the "seigneur" (government); all governments need some source of income. But does it make sense to allow any Tom, Dick or Harry to walk into the mint with 50 cents worth of silver and walk away a week later with a dollar coin? In 1792, Congress seems to think so. Section 14 of the 1792 mint law requires the mint to coin any bullion that private persons might present to it. The first Government anti-poverty program: take some silver bullion to the mint and double your money!

In 1792, Congress does not give the mint money to buy bullion, but simply directs the Secretary of Treasury to make funds available periodically so that the mint can buy bullion. Treasury Secretary Alexander Hamilton never does so, President Washington having put his enemy, Secretary of State Thomas Jefferson, in charge of the mint. Perhaps Washington did this because he had put the Post Office under Hamilton. In one of his last acts on leaving office January 31, 1795, Hamilton proposes that the Treasury assume control of the mint and State take over the Post Office.[4]

In 1814, Britain adopts a gold standard such as had prevailed in earlier periods (e. g. the Roman Empire). Given Britain's importance in the world economy, the gold standard,

4. By the 1830's, several laws change this, placing the Mint under the Treasury (Mint Acts, 4 Stat. 774, and 5 Stat. 136).

i. e. gold "mono-metallism," gradually spreads to other European countries. Remember here the terms "gold standard," and "mono-metallism" as opposed to "bi-metallism."

Whatever the reason, by refusing in the 1790's to give the mint money to buy bullion, Hamilton makes the mint dependent on private persons to bring in precious metals to be turned into gold and silver coins. This situation helps anchor in American psychology the idea of "free coinage." It certainly puts the volume of coinage outside government control.[5] In the 19th century, silver miners demand such "free coinage." What they get is something else: the government undertakes to buy, at varying times, a certain amount of silver each month at market prices. Recall that for years from the 1930's, most American farmers enjoyed a government guaranteed, often above-market price for their products. So what's so strange about government support for hard-pressed silver miners in the 1890's? The analogy between current government agricultural price supports, and 19th century government support of the silver price shouldn't be pushed too far. The "family farmer," in whose name the 20th century government price supports are designed, evokes much more sympathy than any mythical 19th century "family silver miner." Remember here: government support for silver miners.

You are now up to speed on the basics of the nation's money, precious metals, and government support for silver.

---

5. The Federal Reserve now closely watches the nation's money supply, and tries to fine tune it.

CHAPTER TWO

WHO IS PORTER NELSON?

c. 1886

Porter Nelson's story from adulthood on weaves in and out of the following pages. But no one springs full blown on this earth without inherited baggage. Not even some who, like Porter Nelson, falls far from the tree. To understand his life, we must know something of his origins.

William Porter Nelson is a Civil War baby, born in Culpeper, Virginia on August 26, 1862. Just days before, General Robert E. Lee ends a brief, but harsh occupation of the town by Union General Pope. Then when Porter is one year old, Union troops retake Culpeper, with George Armstrong Custer leading the charge. The Confederates never come back in force.

Nelson's parents are Lewis Porter Nelson and his third wife, Mary Elizabeth nee Grinnan. Lewis Porter Nelson is a successful merchant, banker and investor in land (the listing of his land sales fills pages 202 to 208 in the Grantor Index to Culpeper County deeds for 1749 to 1913). He escapes Civil War service by hiring a substitute; his business continues as Culpeper changes hands. His marriage to Mary Elizabeth is very productive, with nine children born between 1859 and 1875. As a child, Porter Nelson attends several private schools. In 1876, he is at the Wheatdale Classical Academy, a 5-day a week boarding school on a farm one mile outside Culpeper preparing boys for college, teaching or business. In 1877, he attends the Culpeper Male Academy. I do not know how long he is there, or what he does up to 1880, when he enters Roanoke College in Salem, Virginia. Before Porter, half-brother Mortimer, and after Porter, younger full brothers George and Arthur, also go to Roanoke College. Sister Kate goes to the Episcopal Institute for Women in Winchester, Va.

As the oldest surviving son of a successful businessman, Porter Nelson could look forward to an easy life in Culpeper, without financial hardship. But at age 24, he leaves Virginia. What really moves him leave Virginia is not clear from the historical record. But it is his departure from comfortable Culpeper to take on the challenge of the West, with all the attendant risks, that inspires my telling of his life story.

CHAPTER THREE

THE WAY TO ASPEN

May 10, 1872 A new mining law is enacted. The Mining Act of 1872 (17 Stat. 91) opens public lands to mineral exploration and purchase by citizens, or intending citizens. Under it, a person who locates a valuable mineral on public land can purchase up to 20 acres of mineral land, plus an adjoining 5 acres of non-mineral land, for $5.00 an acre. The price set by this law (unchanged today) is incredibly low by present standards. But remember, the law is intended to encourage development, and the per acre price is more than 200 times what the US paid Russia for Alaska in 1867. When the law passes, the price of silver bullion is $1.32 an ounce; it will drop steadily after passage of the Act.

February 12, 1873 Congress passes the Coinage Act (17 Stat. 424) mandating the minting of a curious coin known as the Trade Dollar. This dollar has 420 grains of standard silver vs. 412 ½ grains in the standard dollar no longer to be minted. The heavier silver content will make the trade dollar competitive in the Far East with the Mexican dollar. Intended just for export, it is made legal tender in the US!

July, 1873 Financed by a $75,000 appropriation by Congress, three parties organized by Ferdinand V. Hayden of the US Geographical and Geological Survey set out from Denver to conduct a systematic resource survey of Colorado. The so-called Middle Division party covers the eastern approach to Aspen. Hayden's subsequent report to the Secretary of Interior (vol. 6 of the series of Hayden's annual reports) gives an altitude of 7,942 feet for the site of the future town of Aspen at the junction of Castle Creek with the Roaring Fork River. The survey parties return to Denver at the end of October, their field work over for the season.

<u>July, 1874</u> Three parties from the US Geographical and Geological Survey again set out from Denver to extend their systematic survey of Colorado. This year, the Elk Mountains west of Aspen (including such peaks as Sopris, Snow Mass, Maroon and Crested Butte) will be studied by the Middle Division party. Hayden's report (volume 7 of his annual reports, published in 1876) thanks several area railroads for giving the survey parties half price tickets, and the Indian Agent at the Los Pinos Ute Agency. The agent probably cleared the survey work with the Utes. The Middle Division party completes work and returns to Denver November 10.

<u>January 14, 1875</u> The Specie Payment Resumption Act (18 Stat. 296) comes into force, by which the United States extends gold backing to all US currency. This step is designed to make <u>all</u> US paper currency respectable, particularly the fiat Greenbacks issued in the Civil War.

<u>August 1, 1876</u> Colorado joins the Union as the 38th state. Colorado recognizes US ownership of untitled land in the state, in accordance with precedent.

<u>Summer, 1877</u> A silver mining boom hits Leadville on the eastern slope of the Continental Divide, outside Ute territory.

Leadville is just 40 miles from the future Aspen, and becomes the base for future prospector forays into the Aspen area.

February 6, 1878 The New York Times reports that England and Germany have sent $60 million of US bonds to be redeemed, costing the US that much in gold to pay off the bonds. Since Europe still holds some $300 to $500 million in bonds, many fear a run on US gold if Congress passes pending bills on requiring government silver purchases.

February 28, 1878 Congress passes the Bland-Allison Coinage of Silver Act (20 Stat. 25), over the veto of President Hayes. Section 1 of the Act mandates renewed minting of standard silver dollars (none had been minted since 1853) and Treasury purchase of $2-$4 million worth of silver a month for this coinage. The Treasury in practice never buys more than the $2 million minimum in any month. Section 2 of the Act requires the President to convene an international conference (a) to seek agreement on a common silver-to-gold ratio, and (b) to promote bi-metallism in currencies.

June 28, 1878 Delegates to the coming Paris Bi-metallic Congress demanded by the Bland-Allison Act meet with Secretary of State Evert. The US hope: to induce European countries to increase silver use in their monetary systems.

August 16, 1878 The Bi-metallic Congress opens in Paris. The US proposes that, where unrestricted coinage of silver exists, such coinage should be kept as legal tender. Where silver coinage has been stopped, it should be resumed. And the countries should agree on a proper silver-to-gold ratio.

<u>August 30, 1878</u> The International Bi-metallic Congress ends, saying that while no agreement was reached, the discussions held have increased understanding of the silver question.

<u>Summer, 1879</u> Prospectors enter the Roaring Fork valley, some from Leadville, crossing over Independence Pass. They have the maps prepared by the Hayden party. On return to Leadville, a few bring tales of good silver prospects.

<u>September, 1879</u> On September 10, the Indian Agent to the White River Utes, Nathan Meeker, writes Colorado Governor Pitkin that the Indians had assaulted and driven him from his house. Meeker later dies at Indian hands, but is immortalized by having a town named for him. In October, an Army major and 12 men are wiped out by the Indians. Governor Pitkin urges an aggressive campaign against the White River Utes. Chief Ouray of the southern (Uncompahgre) Utes goes to Washington to help make peace.

<u>Fall, 1879</u> Henry B. Gillespie comes into the Roaring Fork Valley from Leadville, organizes the prospectors in the valley into a mining camp called Ute City. The organization he sets up, while not meeting the full requirements of Colorado law for a town, has priority under Federal land regulations for obtaining a patent for a town site. He returns to Leadville and goes East to raise money to develop the enterprise. In Cincinnati and Philadelphia, he finds willing investors. In the latter city, he forms the Roaring Fork Development Company. The Company plans a toll road into the Ute City mining camp from Buena Vista in the Arkansas River valley.

<u>February 6, 1880</u> Just an amateur at surveying, promoter B. Clark Wheeler persuades the Surveyor General of Colorado to give him a commission to carry out a survey of the future Aspen town site. He struggles through the winter snow into the Roaring Fork valley from Leadville.

<u>March 16, 1880</u> The Agent at the Los Pinos Indian Agency in Colorado sends a telegram to the Department of Interior warning that many prospectors were trespassing on the reservation allotted to the Ute tribe, and that more trespassers on the reservation could be expected seeking to locate mining claims or take up ranches. The Department of the Interior gives notice, little heeded, that lands within the Ute reservation (which extends to the western approach to the future town of Aspen) are not part of the public lands of the United States. Such lands therefore are not subject to claim, under the 1872 Minerals Act, the 1862 Homestead Act, or otherwise. Chief Ouray, the senior Ute chief then in Washington concluding an agreement by which the Utes would quit their Colorado reservation, hurries home to head off trouble between the Utes and white would-be miners and ranchers. He is such a valuable peace maker that Washington is paying him $1,000 a year. Ouray dies before the agreement is carried out.

<u>March 26, 1880</u> B. Clark Wheeler files with the Land Office in Leadville a certificate that he has faithfully and accurately surveyed the exterior boundaries of the Aspen town site. This survey will turn out later to be inaccurate, and the patent issued thereupon will be canceled. Wheeler, like Gillespie, goes east, and there incorporates the Aspen Town and Land Company.

Political conventions, 1880 The Republican party holds its convention in Chicago, and names James A. Garfield as its candidate. Silver is not yet a big issue. Also meeting in Chicago, the Greenback Party names James B. Weaver of Ohio as its candidate for President. He runs on a platform calling for repeal of the Specie Payments Resumption Act. The Greenback platform also calls for ending the sale of bonds to finance silver purchases under the Bland-Allison Act. The Greenbackers charge that such purchases only enrich the owners of silver mines. The Democrats meet in Cincinnati and name Winfield S. Hancock as their Presidential candidate. Their platform is silent on the silver question.

Summer, 1880 The Colorado legislature attaches to Gunnison County the settlements in the Roaring Fork Valley (which will get the names of Independence, Ashcroft, Aspen).

August 27, 1880 The US Land Office in Leadville publishes a notice of B. Clark Wheeler's filing of an application for the patent of the Aspen town site. It calls for persons opposing the application to appear at a hearing on October 12, 1880.

August 28, 1880 Telegrams come to the Department of the Interior in Washington reporting that 75 Utes of the southern bands have ratified the Washington agreement on their resettlement. The Indian agent expresses the opinion that the death of Chief Ouray will not prevent the southern Utes from accepting the agreement. This despite the fact that about 40% of the reservation given the Utes in the Conejos Treaty of 1868 is being taken back by Washington. The Utes have been moved around a lot, first by the Mormons in Utah who confined Utah Utes to the Uintah lands in Eastern Utah. In

1861, President Abraham Lincoln in an Executive Order recognized this Uintah reservation for the Utes.

October 2, 1880 A Commissioner appointed to deal with Utes arrives back in Washington with the signature of 577 Ute Indians ratifying the agreement concluded in Washington in March. The task remains of distributing to the various tribal units their shares of the $75,000 promised to the Utes as a whole, and of supervising the removal of the Indians to their new homes. Due to the lateness of the season, the Commissioner says that no Indians can be moved until the following spring.

October 17, 1880 Porter Nelson, who has just entered Roanoke College in Salem, Virginia, joins the Ciceronian Literary Society. Roanoke College, which is in the process of converting from a two year to a 4-year curriculum, gives Nelson the status of a sophomore.

November 2, 1880 Republican James Garfield beats Democrat Winfield Scott Hancock. Republicans control both House and the Senate, but not by large margins. Silver is not yet an issue between the parties.

December, 1880 Porter Nelson becomes Ciceronian Treasurer.

February 21, 1881 The Colorado legislature creates a new county, Pitkin, to include the several Roaring Fork settlements, and makes Aspen the temporary seat. This name, chosen by promoter B. Clark Wheeler, wins out despite Henry Gillespies's work in establishing the Ute City mining camp.

April 22, 1881 Voters in Aspen hold their first municipal election. A newspaper, the Aspen Times, begins publication with election coverage. Two months later, Aspen has another paper, the Rocky Mountain Sun. Aspen is looking up.

May 3, 1881 Porter Nelson is named Secretary of the Ciceronian Literary Society of Roanoke College. Still only 19, he appears for the first time as a buyer of land in Culpeper County, Va. records (deed book 20, page 23). He will next appear as a buyer some years later, once in 1885, and twice in 1886. Years later, from Colorado, he sells Virginia real estate when he is short of money.

May 2, 1881 A German delegate to an international monetary conference in Paris, called by France and the United States, says that Germany will not agree to unlimited silver coinage unless Britain also does so. Later, France shows the conference a new five franc piece, using silver as well as gold. It will replace an entirely gold five franc piece.

June 1881 In Leadville, Colorado, J. W. Deane applies to the US Land Office for a patent on the Aspen town site, signing the application as a Judge (appointed, not elected) in the new Pitkin County. He agrees to pay $1.25 an acre for the 255.5 acres of the Aspen town site as shown in B. Clark Wheeler's survey. The application does not show that Deane is also an official in Wheeler's Aspen Town and Land Company and is using funds provided by that Company. It ignores Gillespie's organization of Ute City residents, many of whom have taken already possession of lots. Ute City residents form a Citizen's Protective Association to fight efforts of the Aspen Town and Land Company to take over "their" town.

Meanwhile, in Virginia, Porter Nelson is named to the honor roll of Roanoke College, with no unexcused marks in the first term of the 1880-81 school year, and with no delinquent marks whatsoever for the second term. He also is elevated to Vice President of the Ciceronian Society.

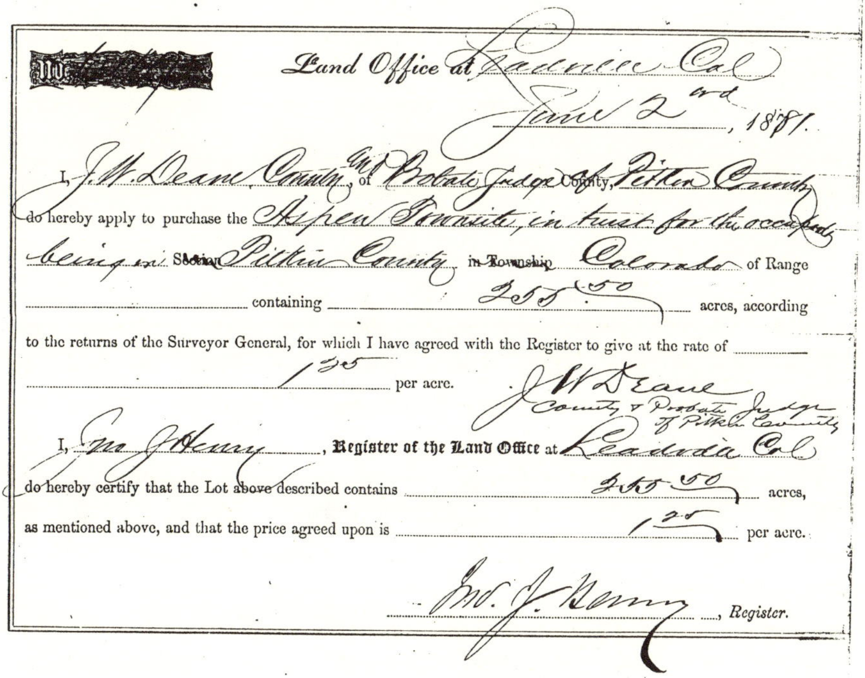

No.

Land Office at Leadville Col

June 2nd, 1881.

I, J. W. Deane County and Probate Judge of County, Pitkin County do hereby apply to purchase the Aspen Townsite, in trust for the occupants being in Section Pitkin County in Township Colorado of Range containing 255.50 acres, according to the returns of the Surveyor General, for which I have agreed with the Register to give at the rate of 1.25 per acre.

J. W. Deane
County & Probate Judge
of Pitkin County

I, Jno. J. Henry, Register of the Land Office at Leadville Col do hereby certify that the Lot above described contains 255.50 acres, as mentioned above, and that the price agreed upon is 1.25 per acre.

Jno. J. Henry, Register.

J. W. Deane's application for the Aspen Town Site Patent

June 6, 1881 The Commissioners appointed to carry out the March, 1880 agreement meet, at the Los Pinos agency in southern Colorado, with Ute chiefs and at least 1,200 armed Utes. The Commissioners state that it is the intention of the government to move the Utes to their new homes as soon as possible. The Commissioners have little reason to expect a joyful occasion; the New York Times describes it as "exciting, dramatic, and perilous in the extreme." Subsequently, 400 Utes move under guard to a new reservation just south of the existing Uintah reservation in Utah. Their deceased chief, Ouray, is "honored" by the name given to their new home.

June 28, 1881 The London Times says Britain accepts the invitation to the International Monetary Conference solely as a courtesy to France and United States. The Times predicts the Conference, if it reconvenes, will immediately adjourn.

July 8, 1881 The International Monetary Conference unanimously adopts a French-American resolution stating that the conference has promoted discussions in and among the states participating, and that the conference will adjourn until April 12, 1882, in the hopes that these discussions on bi-metallism will facilitate reaching an agreement later.

September 4, 1881 Former Secretary of State Evert, named by the wounded President Garfield as the head American delegate to the just ended International Monetary Conference, says on his return to New York that the 1881 Paris Conference was more successful than the 1878 Conference. He adds that setting up an international money system based on both silver and gold could not be done in a brief consultation.

September 19, 1881 The first public school opens in Aspen. Aspen is becoming an established community. Porter Nelson a quarter century later will serve on the Aspen school board.

October, 1881 Porter Nelson, now a member of the senior class at Roanoke College, is elected Ciceronian President.

December 10, 1881 The Aspen Times attacks a town site law passed by the Colorado legislature. The paper says that the law ignores the rights of Aspen citizens under Federal law, and favors the Aspen Land and Town company run by outsiders.

February 22, 1882 The Ciceronian Society holds a celebration to mark Washington's birthday. As Anniversarian, Porter Nelson delivers what the Roanoke Collegian terms an excellent speech on "Virginia," in a "pleasant style."

June, 1882 As a member of the 1882 class, Porter Nelson receives a B. S. degree from Roanoke College; ten men receive degrees this year. Nelson wins the Trustees' Medal in Mathematics. This medal is one of only three handed out. As valedictorian, he delivers a speech on "Problems of the Day." At Roanoke, Nelson belongs to the Ciceronian Society and to Phi Gamma Delta fraternity, but not to the Geological and Mineral Society. Apparently yet to be awakened is his later interest in mining and minerals.

TWELFTH

ANNUAL CELEBRATION

OF THE

CICERONIAN LITERARY SOCIETY.

Wednesday Evening, February 22d, 1882.

"PAX MENTIS INCENDIUM GLORIÆ."

PROGRAMME:

PRAYER BY

Rev. Dr. L. A. FOX.

MUSIC—Selection—"Thoughts of Heaven."

ADDRESS BY THE PRESIDENT,

J. W. CARTER, Henry County, Va.

MUSIC—Quickstep—"Confederation."

FIRST ORATOR.

J. N. ALLISON, Texas.

SUBJECT—"TEXAS AND HER STAR."

MUSIC—Song—"Come Where the Wild Flowers Bloom."

DEBATE:

QUESTION—RESOLVED, "THAT THE SIGNS OF THE TIMES INDICATE A SUBVERSION OF THE GOVERNMENT."

AFFIRMATIVE.

W. D. BOYLE, Kentucky.

MUSIC—Waltz—"Songs from the North."

NEGATIVE.

C. A. MILLER, Virginia.

MUSIC—"Poco Polka."

ANNIVERSARIAN,

W. P. NELSON, Virginia,

SUBJECT—"VIRGINIA."

MUSIC—"Dream on the Ocean Wave."

BENEDICTION.

USHERS.

P. M. RENICK,	CLIVE METCALFE,
S. L. JONES,	E. L. DREHER.

MARSHALS.

D. J. FOLSOM,	T. J. BANDY,
GEO. W. JONES,	JOHN W. PLAINE.

"REGISTER" PRINT, SALEM, VA.

Porter Nelson as Anniversarian

DEPARTMENT OF THE INTERIOR,

WASHINGTON

March 2, 1885

The Commissioner of the
General Land Office,

Sir:

I am in receipt of an application to review my decision of 18th July last in the matter of the Aspen Townsite claim, wherein after finding the facts I directed the patent to issue to the corporate authorities upon the entry already made, Leadville, Colorado, No. 647.

It is alleged (1) that the statement that "claimants under the entry now agree," is incorrect; and (2) that no money was ever paid by the probate judge of Gunnison County, when presenting the original application.

It is only necessary to say that according to my personal recollection the understanding of the parties was strongly urged verbally before me; also that the finding vas qualified by the statement that appeal had "been waived by the present county judge." These were sufficient grounds for my action, and even had no consent been given, I should have made the same direction in the case as an award upon the merits.

That the money was in the hands of the officers sufficiently appears, also that it was in the first instance tendered in support of the application.

I accordingly direct that patent issue in conformity to my decision.

Very respectfully,

H M Teller

Secretary.

Vol.4, No.680 1-2.

Secretary Teller's Aspen town site decision

<u>September, 1883</u> B. Clark Wheeler takes over as editor and publisher of the <u>Aspen Times</u>, succeeding D. H. Waite. Waite wants to devote more time to his law practice. A meeting of Aspen citizens approves the outlines of a settlement of the long dispute with the Aspen Land and Town Company over town lots. The settlement envisages that those residents who have made improvements will receive lot titles at a cost of only about $8 for title work. The city will receive title to four square blocks that it has claimed, and also to 50 other lots. The town site company will take uncontested title to the remaining land within the town boundaries, and will pay all further legal costs. The company clears the prior claims of three men who had established ranches at the Aspen town site before it was staked out. But town site problems continue.

<u>Political conventions, 1884</u> The Republicans convene in Chicago in June, and name James G. Blaine of Maine as their candidate for President. Silver is not a big issue. In July, the Democrats meet, also in Chicago, and nominate Grover Cleveland, ex-Governor of New York, as their candidate for President. Silver does not figure in the Democratic platform.

<u>July 18, 1884</u> Is the town site battle now nearing an end? Secretary of the Interior Henry M. Teller, a past and future Colorado Senator, rules that Pitkin County Judge J. W. Deane, who applied for the Aspen town site patent in Leadville in 1881, was legally qualified to do so. Big New York investor Jerome B. Wheeler starts up Aspen's first operating smelter. The smelter reduces 30 tons of ore a day, eliminating the least valuable 9/10ths. It costs $80 a ton to haul ore by team from Aspen to Leadville. Large scale mining

is hardly economic in the area if low value material must be hauled by team across the mountains.

October 28, 1884 In Virginia, Porter Nelson takes the oath as 2nd Lieutenant, Company B (Culpeper Minutemen), 3rd Infantry Regiment, Virginia Volunteers.

November 7, 1884 Democrat Cleveland wins the Presidential election. Democrats keep control of the House, but fail to win the Senate. Aspen is booming; it will have a total of 1,000 houses by the end of the 1884 season, although many of these are the simplest sort of house for miners.

November 28, 1884 A new town site move. Instructions are issued by the Commissioner of the General Land Office that the patent for the Aspen town site should specify that it does not convey title to any mine of gold, silver, cinnabar, copper, or to any pending valid mining claim.

March, 1885 Interior Secretary Teller settles, at last, the long dispute over the Aspen town site. He directs the Commissioner of the General Land Office to issue the town site patent based on J. W. Deane's 1881 application. Teller must hurry. In 18 days, Republicans of Chester A. Arthur's Administration will be replaced by Grover Cleveland's Democrats. The patent is issued the next day. Aspen mines are now producing over $10 million of ore a year. By the end of the summer, 1,000 tons of freight a week are hauled by team to and from Aspen.

May, 1885 President Grover Cleveland sends former World editor Manton Marble to Europe to explore possibilities for an international agreement on establishing a bi-metallic standard.

At the 1878 and 1881 conferences, Britain and Germany had blocked agreement. Is Aspen the leading edge of technology? On May 19, the Aspen Electric Light and Power Company begins electric service to 40 stores in town. Later, the Spar Consolidated Mine installs Aspen's first telephone, to connect the mine to the home of the mine doctor. By end of the school year, Aspen's single school house, designed for 150 students, will have an enrollment of 175. Construction begins on a new school building. Good thing; a year later, Aspen school enrollment is over 300.

<u>January 1, 1886</u> As many as 70 teams of four horses each are carrying about 15 tons a day across the range to the Arkansas River valley or Leadville for the Aspen Mining and Smelting Company. Since September 9, 1885, such teams have hauled over 4.6 million pounds of freight from Aspen.

<u>March 20, 1886</u> In Washington, a debate opens in the House on a bill submitted by Representative Bland of Missouri for the free and unlimited coinage of silver (in April, it will be defeated by a 163 to 126 vote). Another bill to stop purchases under Bland-Allison Act unless silver is remonetized by international agreement by July 1, 1889 is then defeated decisively, largely by Republican votes.

<u>July 9, 1886</u> The self-appointed International Bi-Metallic League issues a statement at its meeting in Cincinnati terming the Bland-Allison Act a failure after eight years of trial. The League urges the United States to stop coining silver dollars, and to seek an international agreement on "restoring both gold and silver to their proper places as full legal tender money, with free coinage."

September, 1886 At the urging of the Indian Government, the UK sets up a Royal Gold and Silver Commission to study the use of these metals in the currencies of the world.

Early, 1887 Many months before this, the Atchison, Topeka and Santa Fe Railroad decided to build its own 116-miles standard gauge line north from Pueblo into Denver in lieu of using a third rail on the roadbed of the Rio Grande Railroad. In 1886, the Santa Fe formed a subsidiary to build the line. I don't know how he heard about the project, or when he left Virginia, but Nelson is now working with the survey party for this new line. He saves a draft for 97 cents issued by the Santa Fe Railroad in Pueblo, in February, 1887, marked "in payment of Jany salary." A paltry amount, raising questions: did he save the draft because it was his last Santa Fe wage payment? If so, how long had he worked for the Santa Fe?

March, 1887 Coinage of the trade dollar is ended by the Trade Dollar Retirement Act (24 Stat. 634). These dollars, first coined in 1873 and containing more silver than the standard dollar, were coming back to the U. S. and causing confusion. The Mint begins turning out standard silver dollars again, known as Morgan dollars.

June 8, 1887 The New York Stock Exchange begins trading in "silver bullion certificates." The certificates represent bullion held in the vaults of New York's Mercantile Safe Deposit Company in the form of silver bars of a fineness not less than 998 and a weight not greater than 1,200 ounces. The Exchange says these silver bullion certificates are intended to facilitate trade by American companies with silver standard countries, allowing them to fix firm prices as trades are made, rather than taking their chances by settling later through London, as has been practice heretofore. In effect, the certificates facilitate speculation on the silver price.

November, 1887 Hurriedly building a narrow gauge line up the Roaring Fork valley from Glenwood Springs, the Denver and Rio Grande opens the first rail service ever to Aspen. During its first 45 days of operation, the Rio Grande hauls out about 400 tons of ore a day. A second railroad company, the Colorado Midland, pushes standard gauge tracks into Aspen less than 90 days later, its route crossing the Continental Divide by Hagerman Pass and into the drainage of the Frying Pan River. The availability of rail transport makes many mining claims economic for the first time. Of the 200 or so mines operating around Aspen up to now, fewer than ten are really profitable. Rail service means serious competition to the teams hauling goods over the mountains to a distant railhead, but teams still have a monopoly on hauling ore into Aspen from outlying mines. Also subject to competition: the smelter that in 1884 transformed Aspen. Aspen ore can now be treated in many other places. Porter Nelson is back in Virginia. He serves as best man in a Culpeper wedding and becomes an Enrolled Apprentice at Culpeper's Fairfax Lodge no. 43 of the Free and Accepted Masons. He meets Julia Henry Blackwell, through a somewhat younger Culpeper friend, Fayette Latham. Latham, who was studying medicine in Baltimore, marries Julia's sister Annie there on November 3.

December 11, 1887 The President sends to Congress the October 1, 1887 report of Edward Atkinson. Atkinson had been sent to Europe by Secretary of State Bayard to explore possibilities for an international agreement on the proper silver-to-gold ratio. Atkinson reports: "I am convinced by my own observations, sustained by the judgement of other United States citizens or officials, that it would be unwise and inexpedient for the United states to again take the initiative" to secure such an agreement. The United States is burdened with silver dollars it can not get into circulation. The 16:1 silver-to-gold ratio used in the United states is at variance with the ratio used by all other countries. In Colorado, Governor Pitkin calls for removing all Ute Indians from his state into Utah.

February 18, 1888 Porter Nelson records his first purchase of Aspen real estate: Lot D, Block 90 in downtown Aspen. By August 15, 1888, he records eight more lot purchases, two chattel loans (one to J. M. Stewart), and posts a bond for, and receives, a commission as a notary public.

June, 1888 The major political parties hold their conventions. The Democrats meet first this year, in St. Louis. They renominate Grover Cleveland. The principal planks of the Democratic platform are directed (a) against excessive taxation and the revenue surplus of $60 million annually run up by the Republicans, and (b) against centralization of power in the Federal Government. Nothing is in their platform on silver. Meeting later, in Chicago, the Republicans make William Henry Harrison their Presidential nominee. The Republican platform focuses mostly on raising a higher protective tariff, but also condemns Democratic efforts in Congress to demonetize silver. Note that the Republicans at this point are for high taxes (duties) and are silver's friend! Times change.

September - October, 1888 In Aspen, the cornerstone is laid for a new Pitkin County courthouse. In Baltimore, W. Porter

Nelson marries J. Henry Blackwell. After a three weeks' honeymoon, the bridal couple are "at home" for three days at the Carmer residence, 104 W. North Avenue, Baltimore. Then the pair is off to Aspen, where one of the city's periodic outbreaks of scarlet fever awaits them.

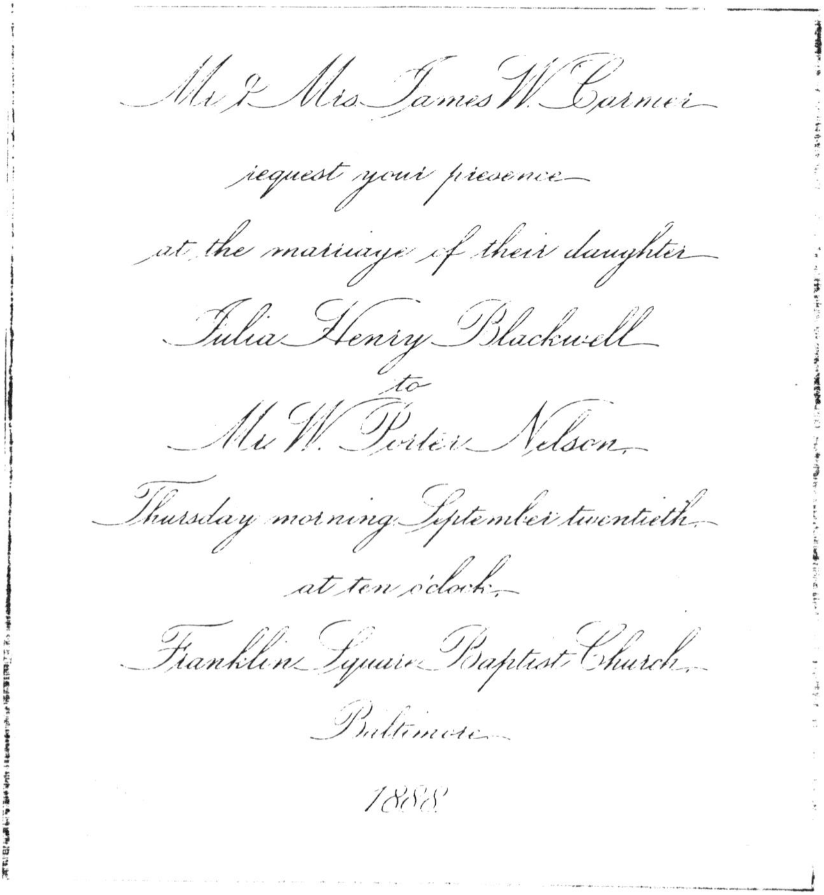

Mr & Mrs James W. Carmer
request your presence
at the marriage of their daughter
Julia Henry Blackwell
to
Mr W. Porter Nelson
Thursday morning September twentieth
at ten o'clock
Franklin Square Baptist Church
Baltimore
1888

November 6, 1888 Republican Harrison defeats the incumbent Democratic President, Grover Cleveland. The Democrats lose not only the White House, but also their control of the House. Republicans continue their long hold on the Senate. The Republican's main goal is to raise tariffs to protect Northern industry. They realize that the votes of the silver bloc will be needed for this. In Aspen, Jerome B. Wheeler, Henry P. Cowenhoven and David R. C. Brown, the town's wealthiest citizens, build an aerial tramway up Aspen Mountain to move 2,000 tons of ore a day from the Aspen mine to an ore storage area along the rail road below.

December 2, 1888 The annual report of the Director of the US Mint values the US production of gold in calendar 1887 at $33 million; that of silver, at $53.4 million. World coinage of precious metals in 1887 is estimated at $125 million in gold, and $161 million in silver. The Director says that world gold production has been holding steady, but that world silver production has increased $25 million in four years. The US accounts for a large part of the silver increase. Left unsaid is what is dictated by the inexorable law of supply and demand: increasing production of silver will perforce drive down the price of silver, barring new uses for that metal.

Year end, 1888 Silver mining in Aspen is in full swing. Ore shipments average 2,700 tons a week. But the price of silver now is only 93 cents an ounce, down by 1/3 since passage of the 1872 Mining Act. Is it really a good time for Porter Nelson to invest in Aspen?

CHAPTER FOUR

THE SALAD YEARS

April 23, 1889 Jerome B. Wheeler opens his new opera house in downtown Aspen.

May 1, 1889 The mining superintendent at Aspen's richest mine, the Mollie Gibson, displays a 3' x 2' x 2' chunk of ore assaying 6,000 ounces of silver a ton. This is part of the mine company's drive to boost the price of its stock when shares are sold.

June 28, 1889 In Aspen, Julia Henry presents Porter Nelson with their first child, James Carmer, named after her stepfather, James W. Carmer.

September 7, 1889 In Aspen, plans are announced for a street railway. Free home mail delivery starts.

November 27, 1889 Jerome B. Wheeler opens the doors of his Hotel Jerome, arguably the finest between Denver and San Francisco. Aspen now has 137 telephones. Quite a town.

December 3, 1889 President Harrison delivers his State of the Union message to Congress, but as usual, not in person. He follows Thomas Jefferson's custom, sending his Executive Secretary to Congress, at noon on December 3, to deliver to the House and Senate copies of his message. The reading of the message by the clerk of each body takes about two hours. The main thrust of Harrison's message is to call for a tariff to protect, as he said, all sectors of the population. Under the Bland-Allison Act, the price of silver has now declined to 1/20 that of gold (vs. the official 16 to 1 ratio). Harrison knows that sixteen or so Western Senators hold the balance of power on tariff matters. So he cautiously says: "I have always been an advocate of the use of silver in our currency. We are big producers of that metal and should not discredit it." An enigmatic statement, giving hope to each side of the silver issue. In Aspen, horse-drawn street cars begin to roll; the fare is five cents.

December 6, 1889 In Culpeper, Virginia, the Fairfax Lodge raises Porter Nelson to the rank of Master Mason. He still cherishes his Virginia ties.

April 19, 1890 Mining claims filed since 1880 show that the 1880 Aspen town site survey by B. Clark Wheeler is faulty. Frank D. Howe, City Engineer of Aspen, begins a 6-week resurvey of the site to determine its proper boundaries.

June 7, 1890 The so-called Sherman Silver Purchase Act passes the House. Introduced by a Republican representative from Ohio, John Sherman, the bill is backed by representatives of the western states. As a quid pro quo for western support of the McKinley Tariff, forces wanting a higher tariff support the silver bill. Speculators in the US and abroad try, but fail, to drive up the silver price to the key $1.29 an ounce level.

June 13, 1890 In Denver, R. C. Humphrey, Surveyor General for Colorado, approves Aspen City Engineer Howe's resurvey of the Aspen town site. The Surveyor General sends an approved copy of the new survey to the Mayor of Aspen, for him to take necessary action with the Land Office in Glenwood Springs to secure a corrected land patent.

June 17, 1890 A bill allowing free coinage of silver passes the Senate, with 28 Democrats for and only three against. Fifteen Republicans also vote for, and 21 against.

June 27, 1890 In passing the Dependent Pension Act (26 Stat. 182), Congress allows the Harrison Administration to pump up the US economy. The Act increases the number of Civil War pensioners by 50%, and the amount of pensions paid out by 60%. By thus reducing surplus funds in the Treasury, Republicans undermine Democratic criticism that Republican favor "taxation in excess of need." How the party roles differ between the 1890's and 1990's!

July 4, 1890 In an editorial, the New York Times warns that the silver state Republicans, who joined with the Democrats to pass the Free Coinage bill, could join with the same allies to defeat other legislation desired by Harrison.

July 7, 1890 Six Republican "Silver Bloc" Senators join with Democrats in the Committee on Finance to block consideration of the McKinley Tariff Bill. The same coalition of forces defeats a bill calling for an end to Government silver purchases. "Silver Bloc" Republicans show that they can control the Senate when they join with the Democrats.

July 10, 1890 Although urged by some to support the free coinage of silver, the Senate adopts a silver bill differing from the Sherman Act passed by the House. Two days later, the House accepts the Senate changes. The Sherman Silver Purchase Act (26 Stat. 289) requires the Treasury to buy 4.5 million ounces of silver a month, paid for by new Treasury certificates. The certificates are redeemable at Treasury option in either silver or gold. The 4.5 million ounces is almost the entire output of the western silver mines. The Treasury may take enough production off the market to hold up the silver price. In Aspen, Porter Nelson's decision to invest in silver looks good. But will this last?

August 8, 1890 For what it's worth, the decennial Federal census counts 8,808 souls in Pitkin County, including Aspen.

August 22, 1890 Secretary of State Blaine writes the President that a severe money shortage threatens, caused by many exporters rushing goods to the country to get the goods through Customs before the higher tariff rates take effect.

September 5, 1890 The Atchison, Topeka and Santa Fe pays $2 million in cash and $4.4 million in stock for the Colorado Midland Railroad, one of two lines serving Aspen. It's hubris.

October 1, 1890 President Harrison signs the McKinley Tariff Act (26 Stat. 567), named for Ohio Representative (and future President) William McKinley. The Act levies higher duties on imported goods than ever before. The balance-of-power-holding "Silver Bloc" Senators, by this time supporting the tariff bill, make passage possible. They thus repay their debt to the high tariff forces which had backed government silver purchases. Meanwhile, a strike of railroad switchmen in Denver halts ore shipments from some Aspen mines. Several large mines are forced to stop production.

November 4, 1890 The McKinley Tariff causes a rapid rise in prices. Instructed by Democrats, the general public blames the Republicans. In off-year elections, Republicans lose control of the House of Representatives, but hang on in the Senate.

<u>November 15, 1890</u> New York financiers are alarmed, at least for a period, by the collapse of Baring Brothers Bank in London, after an Argentine company goes bankrupt and fails to make payments to Barings. Barings has brought much English capital into various American railroads, including the Colorado Midland, where two Barings sit on the Board. In the end, the Bank of England bails out Barings (by contrast, in 1995, the Bank of England let Barings fail when a young trader in Singapore gambled away all of Barings capital).

<u>December 20, 1890</u> For the first time since going to Colorado, and the last time ever, Porter Nelson buys land in Culpeper County, Va. (deed book 24, page 124). Is he hedging his bet on silver by reinvesting in Virginia?

<u>January 3, 1891</u> Two Denver men come to the Philadelphia Mint with a 515-ounce brick of silver and a written demand that, pursuant to the Constitution, the silver be coined for them. The Superintendent of the Mint refuses in writing, saying that such private coinage would violate Mint laws and regulations. The men then vow to take the case to the Supreme Court, saying that Congress has no right to demonetize silver or limit its use as legal tender.

<u>January 6, 1891</u> The Director of the US Mint explains his refusal to coin the silver brick. He says that the Mint has only such authority to buy bullion as provided by the Sherman Act. This Act provides that the Mint pay the market price for silver, which now is $1.03. Turning into coin the silver

offered in Philadelphia would mean that the mint was in effect paying $1.29 to buy silver, thus violating the Act.

<u>January 17, 1891</u> Rumors circulate that New York speculators have accumulated a hoard of 12 million ounces of silver, and that some Senators and Congressmen may be involved. The Mercantile Safe Deposit Company of New York has seven million ounces. Guggenheim's Philadelphia Smelting and Refining Company, the Consolidated Kansas City Smelting and Refining Company, and the Lead Trust are said to be among those hoarding silver. Silvermen are skeptical of any scheme to corner the market, saying that the Mercantile hoard belongs to many different persons (no doubt true: the Mercantile company is the depositary for the silver bullion backing the silver certificates traded on the New York Stock Exchange).

<u>January, 1891</u> The Senate passes another free coinage of silver bill, this time by a vote of 39 to 27. Pressure increases on former President Grover Cleveland to speak out on the silver issue. Some of Cleveland's advisers warn him that voicing any anti-silver sentiments again could destroy his chances for gaining the Democratic nomination in 1892.

<u>January 22, 1891</u> The annual report of the Wells Fargo Company gives the following dollar values for US silver and gold production in states west of the Missouri River between 1870 and 1890. Note that silver production more than tripled in just 20 years:

Year	Silver in million$	Gold in million$
1870	17.320	33.750
1871	19.286	34.898

1872	19.924	38.177
1873	27.483	39.907
1874	29.699	38.466
1875	31.635	39.968
1876	39.293	42.587
1877	45.846	44.480
1878	37.248	37.576
1879	37.033	31.470
1880	38.032	32.559
1881	42.988	30.659
1882	48.132	29.011
1883	42.975	27.817
1884	43.530	25.184
1885	44.517	26.394
1886	52.137	29.561
1887	50.839	32.500
1888	53.153	29.988
1889	64.809	32.528
1890	62.931	31.795

<u>January 27, 1891</u> The Director of the US Mint reports that US gold production in 1890 was 1.59 million troy ounces worth $32,845,000, up $45,000 over 1889. The silver output of US mines was 54.5 million ounces, worth (at the average silver price for the year) $57.2 million. This amount of silver, if coined, would yield $70.5 million worth of coins, taking into account normal seignorage. The total amount of silver offered to the Government during 1890 was 68.1 million ounces, of which the Government bought 37.6 million ounces costing $40 million. The Mint Director also stated that in 1891, the Mint turned out more coins than ever before:

gold coins	$20,467,182
silver dollars	$38,043,004
minor coins	$1,884,792

February 10, 1891 On receiving an invitation from E. Ellery Anderson to speak at a Rotary meeting in New York City, Cleveland declines by letter stating that "...It surely cannot be necessary for me to make a formal expression of my agreement with those who believe that the greatest peril would be invited by the adoption of the scheme, embraced in the measure now pending in the Congress, for the unlimited coinage of silver at our mints. If we have developed an unexpected capacity for the assimilation of largely increased volume of this currency, and even if we have demonstrated the usefulness of such an increase, these conditions fall far short of insuring us against disaster if, in the present situation, we enter upon the dangerous and reckless experiment of the free, unlimited and independent silver coinage."

March 18, 1891 One million dollars worth of gold is shipped from New York in the steamship Haval, destined presumably for Germany. When two companies each turn in $500,000 in gold certificates and ask for gold bars for export, the Treasury redeems the certificates, but in gold coins. In 1890, only $250,000 worth of gold coins had been exported, in coin simply because gold was demanded time when the Assay Office which supplies bars was closed. Now Europe wants gold only in the form of bars. To discourage gold bullion exports, the Treasury imposes a surcharge of 40 cents per $1,000 when gold bars are taken for export.

March 20, 1891 The Acting Secretary of the Treasury refuses to answer the hypothetical question whether the Treasury, if asked pay out gold to redeem a silver certificate, would do so. An unnamed official says it would be utterly impossible for the Government to redeem all silver certificates in gold; the Government does not have enough gold to meet its obligations. In an inconsistency not uncommon with Government, he says the Treasury would permit silver certificates to be exchanged for legal tender notes, which in turn could be redeemed in gold. Figure that one out! The New York Times says that the Treasury stock of "free" gold is as low now as at any time in recent years.

March 22, 1891 The New York Times says the Treasury refusal a few days earlier to part with gold bars is causing some alarm. It pokes fun at the explanation of the Director of the Mint for saying that the bars were not released because the transaction was "special" and not "regular." The Times observes that both the Bank of England and the Bank of France had substituted gold coin for bars in sales in the past.

March 23, 1891 The New York Times comments editorially that not long ago, when Grover Cleveland wrote that unlimited coinage of silver would be dangerous, there was a shriek from still solidly Democratic Virginia that Cleveland could not be the Democratic Presidential nominee for 1892. It says that even ex-Governor Hausner of silver state Montana now believes that free coinage of silver would only bring in lots of foreign metal. Best, Hausner argues, to couple free coinage of US silver with a protective duty on imports.

April 23, 1891 Kate Nelson is born in Aspen, Porter and Julia Henry Nelson's second child. She is named after Porter's sister Kate, who died of tuberculosis in 1885. In December, County Clerk Andy Mulqueen enters the birth report into Pitkin County records.

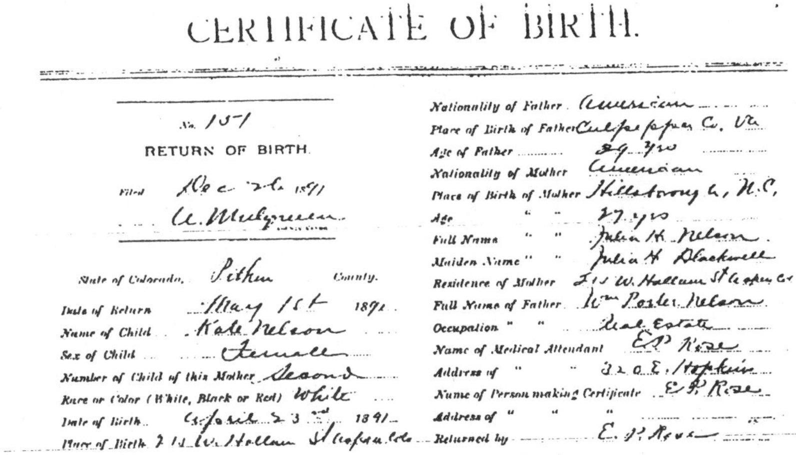

CERTIFICATE OF BIRTH.

No. 151

RETURN OF BIRTH.

Filed Dec 26 1891

A. Mulqueen

State of Colorado, Pitkin County.

Date of Return May 1st 1891

Name of Child Kate Nelson

Sex of Child Female

Number of Child of this Mother Second

Race or Color (White, Black or Red) White

Date of Birth April 23rd 1891

Place of Birth 215 W. Hallam St Aspen Colo

Nationality of Father American

Place of Birth of Father Culpepper Co. Va

Age of Father 29 yrs

Nationality of Mother American

Place of Birth of Mother Hillsborough, N.C.

Age " " 27 yrs

Full Name " " Julia H. Nelson

Maiden Name " " Julia H Blackwell

Residence of Mother 215 W. Hallam St Aspen Co

Full Name of Father Wm Porter Nelson

Occupation " " Real Estate

Name of Medical Attendant E.P. Rose

Address of " " 320 E. Hopkins

Name of Person making Certificate E.P. Rose

Address of " "

Returned by E. P. Rose

The 1891 Birth Record of Kate Nelson

May 10, 1891 New York financial circles are talking about the efforts of European countries to strengthen their gold reserves. Since the first of the year, Europe has taken from the US $35 million in gold. Foreign banks now ask for payment for goods at once in gold. Of course, the high gold outflow reflects in part the accelerated import of goods into the US in advance of the higher McKinley Tariff.

May 17, 1891 US gold exports in the past two weeks total $15 million, the largest ever in a fortnight. Yet money is not tight in the United States; banks are ready to lend, on good collateral at just 5% to 6%, all the money asked for.

June 14, 1891 The Bank of England reportedly is trying to prevent gold from moving back to the United States. But the US will have 160 million bushels of wheat for export this year, for which Europe will pay at least in part with gold.

June 22, 1891 The executive board of the so-called National Committee for Silver, with offices at 1202 Pennsylvania Avenue N. W. in Washington, D.C., meets in New York to plot strategy for a new public campaign for silver coinage. The Committee, headed by General A. J. Warner of Ohio, decides the time is not ripe to arrange a repeat of the St. Louis silver convention of 1890.

August 21, 1891 In Aspen, Julia Henry Nelson's mother, now Mrs. Annie E. Carmer, appears before Porter Nelson, in his capacity of Notary Public, to name a substitute administrator in North Carolina for the estate of Julia Henry's father, Henry Spencer Blackwell. The substitute is to collect moneys due the Blackwell estate under a recent Act of Congress refunding war taxes. The document shows that Porter Nelson's commission as Notary Public expires April 26, 1892.

September 11, 1891 The New York Times says that Treasury collections are below expectations. The work of the War Department is being hindered by a shortage of money, since the Treasury is hoarding cash to redeem an issue of 4 1/2% bonds coming due on October 2. Prudence, not any debt ceiling law, limited government borrowing a century ago.

<u>September 24, 1891</u> A British Board of Trade spokesman, commenting on shipments of gold to America, denies that the Continent will be forced to ship £60 million of gold to the US to pay for grain imports. He says that before as much as £10 million is sent, Britain and France will raise interest rates to stop the drain. He adds that the US is becoming overloaded with £12 million paper currency (silver certificates) annually, and predicts a US crash by February (as it turns out, the crash comes many months later than that).

<u>September 28, 1891</u> Democrat Mills, a candidate for Speaker of the House, terms the silver question secondary to the tariff question. This despite Democratic action in the House passing a free coinage of silver bill. Mills says that Democrats must make the tariff <u>the</u> issue with the Republicans.

<u>September 28, 1891</u> Figures published for the reserves of European central banks show that Britain is the only country to hold no silver reserves whatsoever. Germany and France hold larger gold reserves than Britain. The Germans hold only a small portion of their reserves in silver, while French silver reserves are about the same size as their gold. Netherlands is the only European country whose total reserves fell between 1890 and 1891.

<u>October 1, 1891</u> The New York Chamber of Commerce passes a resolution calling for outright repeal of the Sherman Act requiring Government purchase of 4.5 million ounces of silver a month. In North Carolina, the substitute administrator of the estate of Henry S. Blackwell pays Julia Henry Nelson, her sister and mother the sum of $12. This represents the net refund of war taxes due the Blackwell estate.

<u>October 14, 1891</u> The New York Board of Trade and Transportation calls for the great powers to agree on a proper ratio between the two monetary metals, gold and silver. Any American legislation not in accord with the above ratio will only drive gold out of US currency, the Board says.

<u>November, 1891</u> In St. Louis, proponents of silver coinage hold a convention chaired by A. J. Warner of Ohio. Senator Stewart of Nevada and Representative Bland of Missouri deliver keynote speeches. The convention endorses a platform demanding that the 51st Congress open the US Mint to free and unlimited coinage of silver, which will be legal tender for payment of all debts. In Aspen, the Holden Lixiviation Works begin operations, processing silver ore to reduce greatly the weight the railroads haul out of Aspen. The major Holden investor is from England. The US Land Office in Glenwood Springs receives, from an agent for the Aspen Consolidated Mining Company, applications for mining patents to the so-called Fields, Fowler and Lux gold placers in the Roaring Fork Mining District of Pitkin County. The Aspen Consolidated Mining Company, with offices at 312 E. Cooper, also is seeking patents on its Famous mining property.

<u>December, 1891</u> In Washington, Speaker Crisp of Georgia appoints Missouri Representative Richard Bland as head of the House Banking Committee. Crisp encourages Bland to report out a free coinage of silver bill, partly in the hope of focussing attention on Cleveland's anti-silver stand. This bill is talked to death, but a record vote on it shows that 130 Democrats favor free coinage, while only 80 oppose. In the year 1891, Aspen (with an output of 8.75 million ounces) overtakes older rival Leadville (output 6.11 million ounces) as

the leading silver producer in Colorado. Some say Aspen mines now account for as much as 15% of the world's silver output. The years 1889 to 1891 were good for Aspen, and for Porter Nelson, who is now an established dealer in mines and other investments.

Porter Nelson's business card
(actual size)

CHAPTER FIVE

THE LOOMING CRISIS

January 20, 1892 Wells, Fargo's annual report on North American precious metal production shows that in 1891, the West (including British Columbia) mined $60.6 million of silver, and $32 million of gold. The silver price during the year averages 98 cents an ounce, well below its coinage value of $1.29. California mined the most gold, $10.5 million, and Colorado was second with just under $5 million. Montana was the leading silver producer at $25 million, and Colorado second at $23.5 million. The Aspen City Directory for 1892 shows the Porter Nelson family residing at 215 West Hallam.

February 8, 1892 The Supreme Court of the District of Columbia rejects a suit by persons seeking to compel the Treasury to accept a brick of silver and turn it into coins.

February 20, 1892 The Times notes that gold worth $0.5 million is going to Europe, and three times that amount to go next week. Last year, up to July 24, about $9.3 million in gold bullion left the US for Europe, but payments later in 1891 for US grain exports brought back at least $40 million worth of gold. Is the gold outflow to Europe beginning again?

February 24, 1892 Thomas H. Carter, Commissioner of the General Land Office, writes to his representative in Glenwood Springs pointing out that pending in his office are a number claims under the 1872 Mining Law, and also agricultural claims, which conflict with B. Clark Wheeler's survey of the Aspen town site. The Commissioner states that Aspen town patent should apply to the boundaries of the town site as it exists on the ground, and not as stated in the town site patent based on Wheeler's survey. He suggests that the Glenwood Springs office ask the town authorities to return the original patent so that it can be reissued with a correct description.

March 25, 1892 Representative Bland's bill for free coinage of silver loses in House. Speaker Crisp casts the deciding negative vote, breaking a 148 to 148 tie. In his bill, Bland had made a concession to so-called "scientific bi-metallism" by providing that if France adopts silver coinage at a ratio other than 16 to 1, the US would follow suit. Yet the East and Northeast regions vote solidly against the Bland bill, although it had been devised with an eye to splitting the Republicans.

March 25, 1892 The New York Times cites a broker who says he is receiving many demands from Europe for redemption in gold of solid, old US company bonds which had always paid interest. The European holders had considered them good investments until fears arose that Congress might pass a silver coinage bill.

April 13, 1892 The Land Office in Glenwood Springs informs seven persons whose claims conflict with the Aspen town site patent they have 60 days to appeal the prior town site claims.

May 11, 1892 The British Chancellor of the Exchequer informs proponents of bi-metallism who called on him that England will take part in the conference proposed by the United States. The conference is to consider measures that might be taken to increase the use of silver in the currency systems of the various nations. He says that the British

Government at the conference will consider the statements of large industries that had sent deputations to him, and the interests of India (which operates on a silver standard). Much of the British press is negative about the conference. Remember in 1821, Britain had pioneered the gold standard.

<u>May 16, 1892</u> Germany comes out against bi-metallism. Papers recall that several years ago, the Reichstag had turned down a proposal that Germany agree to negotiate on bi-metallism if Britain first adopts such a policy.

<u>May 31, 1892</u> France agrees to attend the monetary conference promoted by the United States, although Finance Minister Rouvier says that Great Britain, given its responsibility for India, is the European country most affected. Some deputies oppose French participation, saying that Austria was on the verge of making large gold withdrawals from Paris and London. Further, the silver price is declining every day. Minister Rouvier asserts that France, while agreeing to attend, preserves full liberty of action.

<u>May 31, 1892</u> In the House of Commons, a member asks if the US has agreed to give tariff concessions on goods from Sheffield and Birmingham to induce England to attend the monetary conference. A Foreign Office spokesman replies that he has no information on that subject.

<u>June 4, 1892</u> Secretary of the Treasury Foster reports to President Harrison on Foster's talks with financial circles in New York about the coming monetary conference. President Harrison states that the purpose of the Conference is to discuss what measures, if any, could be taken to increase the

use of silver in the currency systems of the various nations. The United States, he says, isn't imposing conditions on the conference that might embarrass any government.

June, 1892 In India, the Council says that if the international conference on silver at Brussels fails, and if India and the United States cannot agree on silver, Indian mints will stop free coinage of silver and India will go to the gold standard.

Political conventions, 1892 As usual, the Republican Party meets before the Democrats, this year in Minneapolis. They renominate Benjamin Harrison for President. Pro-silver delegates win a victory when they secure adoption, in plank no. 1 (tariff), of language attacking the Democrats for putting wool and lead on the duty free list. But the pro-silver people cannot secure clear free coinage language in plank no. 2 (money question). After considerable debate, the Convention adopts the following compromise language on the money question: "The American people, from tradition and interest, favor bi-metallism, and the Republican Party demands the use of both gold and silver as standard money, with such restrictions and under such provisions, to be determined by legislation, as will secure the maintenance of the parity of values of the two metals so that the purchasing and debt-paying power of the dollar, whether of silver, gold, or paper, shall be at all times equal. The interests of the producers of the country, its farmers, and its workingmen demand that every dollar, paper or coin, issued by the government shall be as good as any other . . . We commend the wise and patriotic steps already taken by our government to secure an international conference, to adopt such measures as will insure a parity between gold and silver for use as money throughout the world."

The Democrats meet in Chicago and nominate former President Grover Cleveland for President. The Democratic platform also endorses the use of silver in the currency: "We hold to the use of the both gold and silver as the standard money of the country, and to the coinage of both gold and silver without discriminating against either . . . and we demand that all paper currency shall be kept at par with and redeemable in such coin." The Democratic platform accepts that the parity of the two metals was beyond US control, and provides for this to be "adjusted by international agreement," or by "safeguards of legislation."

In August, the Peoples Party (sometimes called the Populist Party) meets in Omaha and chooses its candidates: for President, James B. Weaver of Ohio, and for Vice President, James G. Field of Virginia. Weaver has already served two terms in the House, and was the Greenback Party candidate in the 1880 Presidential election. The People's Party platform is more outspoken on money than either of the two: "We demand a national currency, safe, sound, and flexible, issued by the general government only, a full legal tender for all debts, public and private, and without the use of banking corporations, a just, equitable and efficient means of distribution direct to the people, at a rate not to exceed 2% per annum, to be provided as set forth by the sub-Treasury plan of the Farmer's Alliance, or a better system, of payments in discharge of obligations for public payments. We demand free and unlimited coinage of silver and gold at the present legal ratio of 16 to 1. We demand that the circulating medium be speedily increased to not less than $80 per capita." Lots of frustration shows through in this platform.

July 14, 1892 The free coinage of silver bill proposed by Senator Stewart of Nevada, which had passed the Senate, is defeated decisively in the House. The Treasury's "free stock" of gold (the amount of gold held over and above the $100 million reserve fund) is now down to $11 million. The "free stock" had been $26 million in January, 1892 and $46 million in January, 1891. New York banks are uneasy and hope the Treasury will find a way of hindering gold bullion exports. Firms wishing to export gold typically buy gold certificates from US banks, and then exchange these at the Treasury for gold bars. To stem the outflow, New York banks reportedly stop selling gold certificates to foreign banks.

July 15, 1892 Two New York bank presidents oppose any suspension of gold payments by the U. S. Treasury. One president says that such a suspension of gold payments would ensure the election of Democrat Grover Cleveland, who had left a $100 million surplus in the Treasury in 1889.

July 18, 1892 The New York Times discusses a private citizen's proposal for taxing silver bullion to raise the price of a silver dollar to parity with the gold dollar. Such a tax would raise the price of the fraction of an ounce silver in a dollar from 70 cents to near the coinage value of $1.29.

August 14, 1892 The New York Times notes that Senator Sherman of Ohio, who gave his name to the silver purchase act, says the law is not been working well and that he now wishes to see it repealed. The Times says that the fall in the price of silver hurts southern cotton farmers by cutting English cotton textile exports to silver currency country India. The certificate of incorporation of the North Pole Mining Company is filed in Pitkin County. Nelson later serves as secretary of the company.

November 8, 1892 Democrat Grover Cleveland, not a silver man, wins the election, defeating incumbent Republican Benjamin Harrison. The Democrats keep control of the House and break the long Republican sway in the Senate. Pitkin County gives 75% of its vote to the People's Party presidential candidate, James B. Weaver. Weaver draws about 10% of the popular vote (Ross Perot got 19% in 1992) and wins 22 electoral votes (vs. Perot's none in 1992). Peoples Party candidates win House seats in Colorado, Idaho, Kansas, Nevada and North Dakota (Perot's party won no seats in 1992).

November 26, 1892 In Brussels, the head of the US delegation at the Brussels International Monetary Conference, Senator Allison, distributes, in French and English, the American proposals. The US believes that the large depreciation of silver compared with gold has hurt commerce the world over, and that international agreement on a fixed parity of silver to gold would be of wide benefit. The US asserts that silver could play a role in the currency of nations, and indeed should be so used to an increasing extent. Allison concedes that the US produces $50 million a year in silver, but points out that total US output is $13 billion. Silver doesn't wag the US dog.

November 30, 1892 At the Conference in Brussels, American bi-metallism ideas do not enjoy wide support. Work continues behind closed doors on the proposal submitted by a British delegate, Alfred de Rothschild. Observers think that an idea is under consideration for increasing national silver purchases over a limited period of something like three years.

December 1, 1892 The New York Times notes editorially that, in the early days of the Harrison Administration, some lesser Treasury officials had said that the Treasury gold reserve of $100 million could be drawn upon to meet any need for which other funds were not available. According to the Times, Secretary of the Treasury Foster has never repudiated such statements, although since 1879 every other Treasury Secretary has considered it imperative to keep the fund intact in order to maintain confidence in the US dollar.

December 5, 1892 In Washington, Congressman George F. Williams denounces the Rothschild proposal made at the International Monetary Conference. He charges that the proposal would require the US to bear the burden of buying 54 million ounces of silver per year, with Europe and India buying only 25 million, if the price doesn't rise above 43 British pence per ounce. He says that a salutary way to end the Brussels conference would be simply to tell the conference that the 52nd Congress, in its remaining three months, would repeal the "monstrous" Sherman Silver Purchase Act.

December 6, 1892 British delegate de Rothschild withdraws his proposal at the Brussels International Monetary Conference. Treasury Secretary Charles Foster submits the report requested by the Senate just before it adjourned the preceding August. The Senate had asked the Treasury to report in what form the Treasury receives payment of Customs duties and internal revenue taxes, whether in gold coin, standard silver dollars, silver certificates, Treasury notes, etc. Foster replies that this information cannot be compiled. He does cite the ratio of gold to silver held in the reserves of European central banks: France (264/252), Germany (168/56), and England (125/10). He adds that the Treasury has taken no action to prevent notes issued under the Sherman Silver Purchase Act from being redeemed in gold. So long as this is the case, he says the US can preserve bi-metallism only by agreement with the other commercial powers.

December 7, 1892 The head of the Butte and Boston Mining Company of Montana proposes to the Secretary of the Treasury that the amount of silver in silver dollar be raised. He points out that, at present prices, a counterfeiter can make a silver dollar using ridiculously little silver: 65 cents worth.

December 9, 1892 If the Brussels conference fails to endorse free coinage of silver, the New York Times says the price is likely to drop further. Below 70 cents an ounce, few silver mines will continue to operate unless they can recover valuable secondary minerals. In Aspen, banks, stores and merchants are steeling themselves for the worst. Aspen is not alone. Towns in Nevada also are losing population. Virginia City formerly had 20,000 people, and mines producing ore worth millions. Now the city's population is 7,000 and many once profitable mines there are running in the red. As a result, the Carson City Mint has little bullion to process. Exhaustion of rich ore, and the falling price of silver are to blame.

December 12, 1892 A New York Times editorial says that the Treasury has issued $378 million in notes to buy silver bullion under Sherman Silver Purchase Act, bullion worth $308 million at the time of purchase. That quantity of silver is now worth only $250 million, or just 70% of the purchase price. In Berlin, Chancellor von Caprivi says that he has sent instructions to the German International Monetary Conference delegates to oppose any limitation on Germany's freedom to decide for itself the content of German currency.

<u>December 12, 1892</u> German exporters take $2.25 million in gold from the US Treasury. French exporters take another $900,000.

<u>December 13, 1892</u> A delegate representing India at the International Monetary Conference in Brussels attacks Britain for failing to contribute to a solution. A British delegate replies that Britain did not send a delegation to discuss bimetallism, a subject not in accord with the purposes of the meeting. Senator Jones of the US delegation argues at length that the fall in the price of silver has disastrous consequences not just for the US but for business everywhere. The US government no longer expects results from the Brussels Conference that the present Congress can consider.

<u>December 15, 1892</u> The committee appointed at the Brussels Conference to produce a final report quits without making any recommendation. Senator Allison promises that if the Conference would only resume its work, the US would be willing to go far to meet the concerns of Europe, conceding that the truest ratio of silver to gold might not be 16:1. The Conference decides to adjourn until June 6, 1893. The London <u>Times</u> castigates the US for calling the conference, then coming with only "platitudes."

December 18, 1892 Treasury Secretary Foster speaks out on concerns being expressed about the outflow of gold from the United States. He notes that he will be in charge of the Treasury until March 4, 1893, and asserts that he will use all resources at his disposal to maintain the parity of silver to gold as required by law. He says the Treasury has the power to sell bonds to buy gold, and that in his annual report to the Congress, he will even recommend increasing the Treasury gold reserve from $100 million to $125 million.

December 19, 1892 Secretary Foster says that while $7 million in gold was shipped out of the United States last month, only $500,000 of that came from the Treasury. He notes the Treasury still holds $24 million in gold over and above the $100 million reserve minimum. He adds that US merchandise trade now is producing a $20 million a month balance in favor of the US, and that Europe will have to send gold to the United States to settle this trade account.

Year end, 1892 Only 200 of 7,000 mineral claims registered in the Aspen district have been patented. Porter Nelson holds one, with seven co-holders (no. 20792, for the Georgiana and five other lodes). In 1895, he (with Jerome B. Wheeler) will become co-holder of another patent (no. 26326 for the Last Chance Lode). Nelson also will become a co-holder of another patent (no. 26785 for the Lucky Queen Lode). Nelson did not discover the lodes. He probably received his ownership interest in them in return for handling the extensive patent paper work (proving the citizenship of patent holders, publishing a notice of patent filing, etc.). When the Land Office found that the Last Chance site survey conflicted with the Bushwhacker claim, the Land Office asked Nelson to correct the former.

CHAPTER SIX

DISASTER

January 1, 1893 As 1893 opens, President-elect Grover Cleveland is at his New York home, preparing for his March 4 inauguration, making no pronouncements. In state capitols, the legislatures are convening which will choose US Senators. Aspen, with an estimated 12,000 residents, may be Colorado's third largest city, preceded only by Denver and Leadville.

January 5, 1893 Representative Andrews, Democrat of Massachusetts, submits a bill to the House Committee on Banking and Currency calling for suspension of silver purchases under the Sherman Act of 1890. His action is prompted by a petition from bank presidents, wool merchants, leather and steel manufacturers, and other public figures in Boston. Senator Hill of New York introduces in the Senate a companion bill to stop silver purchases.

January 6, 1893 Porter and Julia Henry Nelson's third child, Marguerite, is born in Aspen.

January 9, 1893 By a vote of eight to three, the House Committee on Banking and Currency favorably reports out the Andrews bill. It would repeal Section 1 of the Sherman Act, which directs the Treasury to buy 4.5 million ounces of silver a month. The other sections of the Sherman Act remain intact dealing with legal tender status of the notes issued to buy silver, the coinage of $2 million a month, and repeal of the Bland-Allison Act. Committee members who oppose the bill are two Democrats from Kentucky and Tennessee, and one Republican from Colorado. Two Republicans support repeal.

January 9, 1893 In Senate discussion of Senator Hill's bill to stop silver purchases, Senator McPherson argues that silver costs only about 35 cents an ounce to produce. McPherson says this means that the silver in a dollar coin is worth just 25 cents. The government has a higher profit with this coin than any other. Rebutting the argument that farmers would be hurt if silver purchases were stopped, he says that in fact, farmers are cheated when they are paid in dollars really worth only a fraction of a dollar. Further, he charges if the US stays with silver, it will be turning its back on Europe and aligning itself with weaker nations such as India and China. His arguments are interrupted frequently by the leading "silver bloc" Senator, Republican Henry Teller from the gold mining town of Central City, Colorado. Teller asserts that no matter what the Democrats try, the Sherman Act will not be repealed at the present session of Congress.

January 12, 1893 The New York Times quotes ex-Treasury Secretary Charles S. Fairchild as saying that as of January 1, 1893 the Treasury had issued over $1 billion of $1 silver certificates to buy silver under the Sherman Act. These can be kept at par only if the Treasury stands ready to redeem them in gold on demand. Treasury gold stocks continue to fall (e. g. by $1.3 million between January 7 to 21, 1893).

January 16, 1893 Market observers quoted by the New York Times speak of continuing gold exports from the US due to a steady European demand for gold. Porter Nelson sells land in Culpeper County, Va. (deed book 25, page 367).

January 17, 1893 A Senate committee takes up the silver purchase repeal bill introduced the previous July by Senator

Sherman and reports it out favorably. The operative portion of the repeal bill provides that the Treasury will cease buying silver bullion on January 1, 1894. Previously issued silver certificates will remain valid. The New York Times says a friend of Cleveland's will try to get the President-elect to issue a statement on silver before the expiration of present session of Congress. Cleveland has been studying the problem; some think that he favors stopping bullion purchases.

January 18, 1893 A New York Times editorial notes that President-elect Cleveland so far has said nothing on silver.

January 19, 1893 The Times editorially decries the idea of Cleveland calling a special session of the new Congress on silver. It urges the sitting Congress to take a stand on the issue. The editorial does not say what that stand should be, but the views of the Times against silver are well known.

January 20, 1893 A Times editorial quotes other publications to show that the US is losing precious metals. Examples: in 1892, the US exported $70.5 million worth of gold, and imported only $8.5 million worth. The figures for silver were $22.3 million in exports, and $2.8 million in imports.

January 21, 1893 The French liner La Champagne delays its departure from New York by two hours so it can load $3 million of Treasury gold for export to France.

January 22, 1893 The Times says that Democrats have given up hope at this session of getting silver purchase repeal through the Senate. Silver state Senators like Teller and Wolcott of Colorado, and Stewart of Nevada, are ready to filibuster. Of the four territories awaiting statehood (Oklahoma, Utah, New Mexico and Arizona), the latter three are likely to join the silver bloc, if admitted to the Union. The present Congress has only 35 days left to conclude its business; this is hardly enough time to settle the silver question.

January 23, 1893 A New York Times editorial criticizes Senate Republicans for blocking a vote on repeal. It says the House will not take up repeal unless there is a chance that the Senate will act. The Times recalls that Cleveland had set up the $100 million reserve fund, and opines that Cleveland could protect the currency by selling bonds to buy more gold.

January 25, 1893 Prominent New York businessmen sign a petition urging repeal of the Sherman act. The petition notes that the Treasury gold reserve is down to $117 million, against liabilities now seven times that amount. The businessmen think this monetary backing is too thin. They say US issuance of $4 million in silver certificates a month only promotes the export of gold. In an editorial, the New York Times refutes claims of hard times by Colorado silvermen, observing that Colorado silver output increased from 23.1 million ounces in 1891 to 26.45 million in 1892. For the whole country in 1891, the US Mint says silver output was 58.33 million ounces. Of this, the Government bought over 54 million ounces under the Sherman Silver Purchase Act. The Times notes that the government is now paying 84 cents an ounce, whereas it estimates that good mines in Colorado produce ore at 20 cents an ounce of "contained" silver (this estimate doesn't include freight or refining charges). Aspen mines need a much higher silver price than 20 cents.

DISASTER

January 26, 1893 Rumors to the effect that gold worth between $3 and $5 million left the US on Saturday contributes to a bear market for stocks in New York. In a letter to the editor of the New York Times, one I. W. Sylvester of New York says that unless the silver purchase act is repealed in time, the US will not be able to sell bonds to buy gold. The US he writes will then be "in commercial tune with the semi-civilized East Indian races."

January 27, 1893 A Times editorial points out that if the Sherman Silver Purchase Act is repealed and the Bland-Allison Act reinstated (which some are proposing as a compromise), the government will still have to buy $2 million a month worth of silver, causing 2.38 million ounces of bullion to be coined each month into $3.1 million worth of coins.

February, 1893 The US gold loss in 1892 exceeds $50 million. Cleveland mulls calling a special session of Congress immediately after his inauguration for repeal of the Sherman Silver Purchase Act. In the end, he decides to do nothing before his March 4 inauguration. The lame-duck Treasury Secretary prevails upon New York banks to exchange $6 million in gold for Treasury legal tender notes. The Philadelphia and Reading Railroad, with debts exceeding $125 million, goes bankrupt. In Aspen, owners lock out miners to secure a cut in wages. Result: the miners agree to work 10 hours a day for the pay they used to earn in 8 hours.

March 4, 1893 On taking office, Cleveland finds in the Treasury $101 million in gold, but only $25 million in other liquid assets. New Treasury Secretary Carlisle persuades several banks to exchange $25 million more in gold for notes.

DISASTER

April 12, 1893 For the first time since the Treasury set up a gold reserve fund, its value falls below the $100 million target. The Treasury embarks on an emergency program to persuade banks all over the country to turn in gold coins for other forms of currency held by the government. The Treasury also suspends issuance of the gold certificates under the Law of July 12, 1882. People fear that the Treasury may next start paying its obligations in silver only.

April 16, 1893 Julia Henry Nelson is confirmed as an Episcopalian at Christ Church, Aspen, by William Barker, the Missionary Bishop of Western Colorado.

May 4, 1893 The National Cordage Company fails, setting off a widespread decline in stock prices. New York banks begin to refuse to accept notes of banks in the south and west of the country. By the end of the year, 600 banks will fail and two of the biggest railroads, the Union Pacific and the Northern Pacific, will be bankrupt. Panic?

May 8, 1893 Senator Hansbrough of North Dakota charges that greedy Wall Streeters "gather up the paper obligations of the Government and in wild-eyed alarm rush away to the nearest Government Sub-Treasury and demand their redemption in gold . . . The impression that goes out is that a panic is near at hand." Hansbrough is not far off the mark.

June 22, 1893 New York Stock Exchange prices rise when it becomes known that $500,000 in gold is coming from abroad. The Treasury buys 35,000 ounces of silver at 82.2 cents an ounce, and another 65,000 ounces at 82.5 cents, completing its required Sherman Act purchases for June. The Treasury says it will again accept offers of silver on July 3.

June 26, 1893 In India, the Council ends, after 54 years, the free coinage of silver by Indian mints. Ending free coinage of silver is dictated from London; the Financial Secretary for India had opposed the stopping of free coinage unless and until it became clear that the United States would not itself adopt free coinage of silver. The Indian rupee will be valued at 16 British pence and thus be linked to gold. When introduced in 1835 as the standard coin for British India, the rupee was worth two shillings or 24 pence. Massive American silver production has brought down the Indian rupee.

June 29-July 1, 1893 Cleveland calls a special session of Congress to begin August 7 to consider repeal of the Sherman Act, the drain on Treasury gold in the preceding 12 months amounting to $67.5 million. Owners of Colorado and Missouri Valley smelters stop purchases of silver ore. They have five million ounces of silver on hand, more than the Government is obliged to buy in two months' time under the Sherman Act. The price of silver drops to 77 cents an ounce. Many Aspen mines shut down; employment falls sharply, from over 2,000 to one tenth that. Elsewhere employment also falls.

July 15, 1893 The price of silver bars in New York is down to 72 cents an ounce. The Brown Palace Hotel in Denver goes bankrupt.

July 17, 1893 Three large savings banks in Denver close. The next day, the J. B. Wheeler Bank in Aspen closes.

DISASTER

July 22, 1893 There are 10,000 unemployed men in Denver, with more coming to the city from mines closing all over the state. Attendees at a silver convention in Denver say that they can accept repeal of the Sherman Act, if free and unlimited coinage of silver begins. They charge that world capitalists have schemed to demonetize silver, first in Germany, then in several Latin countries, in India and now in the US, with the aim of driving up the value of gold. In Chicago, wheat prices fall below 55 cents a bushel for the first time since before the Civil War. In 1894, corn will fall to 20-30 cents a bushel, cotton to only seven cents a pound. That's deflation.

August 7, 1893 The special session of Congress called by President Cleveland begins debate on Sherman Act repeal.

August 11, 1893 The Aspen Times optimistically reports that silver supporters in the House had met in the chambers of the Judiciary Committee to prepare a pro-silver message. Hunt's, a dry goods store on Hyman Avenue in Aspen, optimistically pays for a first page ad saying that since free-coinage of silver is coming, now is the time to buy.

September, 1893 Many businesses in Aspen move to, or open branches in, the booming Cripple Creek gold mining camp. Aspen newspapers announce that ranchers may now pay for their subscriptions in ranch produce instead of money. The daily wage paid to many miners in Aspen is cut from $3 to $2.25. Porter Nelson raises money by selling land in Culpeper County, Va. (deed book 26, page 18), and by selling a 1/4 interest in his Aspen Block building to banker T. G. Lyster. The year 1893 has not been a good one for him, nor for many others all across America.

DISASTER

November 10, 1893 Congress repeals the Sherman Silver Purchase Act. Spot silver in New York falls to 60 cents.

December 20, 1893 James Grant, owner of one of the largest smelters in Colorado, gives an upbeat assessment of the Colorado economy in a speech at the Manufacturer's Exchange in Denver. He concedes that Colorado silver production will fall, but says silver mining will not be abandoned totally. The fall in the price of silver will redirect efforts to gold mining in the state. He predicts that Colorado gold production in 1893 will be about $2 million higher than in 1892. This means that Cripple Creek will gain as Aspen suffers.

December 30, 1893 The Treasury gold reserve falls to $80 million. The year 1893 has brought hard times for many.

CHAPTER SEVEN

DOWN WITH GROVER

Early January, 1894 As the New Year opens, prices reflect the severe depression that began the previous year. Wheat is selling at an all time low in Chicago of less than 65 cents a bushel. Cotton is selling in New York for less than seven cents a pound. Silverites bemoan the low, 68 cents per ounce price of silver. In Aspen, the Rocky Mountain Sun gloomily notes that many Aspenites are going to the Buena Vista gold fields. Later in the month, the paper describes any Aspen resident who suddenly departs leaving unpaid bills, not as a "failure" but as a "dead beat." The paper contains frequent notices of foreclosure sales.

January 17, 1894 The Treasury wants to sell $50 million in bonds to raise money to buy gold to build up the gold reserve. The Treasury has to make a patriotic appeal to the big banks to subscribe; a number of banks are suffering losses due to the recession. About half the payments for the bonds are made in the form of gold-backed notes. These bring no real strengthening of Treasury gold reserves.

January 13, 1894 Grasping at straws, the Rocky Mountain Sun optimistically tells Aspenites that the Pan-American Bi-Metallic League will meet in Des Moines in February. The League's aim is to help General Weaver promote the election of pro-silver congressmen.

January 18, 1894 The Treasury's gold reserve falls to $69 million, far below the $100 million minimum level.

January 27, 1894 The Sun says that the business depression affects not just Colorado and the US; England, Germany and France also are experiencing hard times. Grasping at any straw, it says foreign countries are now looking at the silver problem and may try to call a new bi-metallic conference. The Sun regrets that the US administration seems content just to sit back and wait. It cites a New York financial letter asserting that confidence in the economy can't be restored until the question of the status of silver is settled.

February 3, 1894 The Sun notes sadly that US has told Belgium it will not reconvene the 1892 Brussels Monetary Conference. The Santa Fe Railroad allows the Midland, one of two rail lines serving Aspen, to go into receivership.

March 3, 1894 Reporting that the silver price is down to 59 cents an ounce, the Sun says that since silver was demonetized, world output of goods has fallen by 1/3 and the US government budget deficit has risen to $72 million. Two major and normally profitable Aspen silver mines, the Aspen and the Durant, are closing or reducing operations.

March 11, 1894 The House passes by 169 to 129 the Silver Bullion Coinage Act introduced by Representative Richard Bland of Missouri. The Act calls for coining $55 million in silver dollars out of bullion already in the Treasury. Only 49 Democrats cast negative votes.

March 29, 1894 Cleveland vetoes the Bland bill calling for the Treasury to coin 55 million silver dollars. In his veto message, Cleveland says that the bill would be a step back from the sound policy adopted by the repeal of the Sherman

Act. Cleveland has already embittered the South and the West; this veto increases the bitterness.

March 31, 1894 The Sun says that Eastern Democrats and the Republicans are preventing New Mexico and the other applicants for statehood from joining the Union simply out of fear their representatives will cast pro-silver votes. It notes that Coxey's Army of the unemployed will be in Washington in May, and says this Army may force Congress to adjourn early. The paper reports that several Aspenites are interested in the mines of the Cochiti, New Mexico gold district. Is everyone quitting Aspen?

April 7, 1894 The House fails to override Cleveland's veto of the Bland bill. The Interstate Bi-Metallic Association meeting in Des Moines claims that 3/4 of the American people want full remonetization of silver. The South Park Railroad, connecting Denver and Leadville, closes after the Union Pacific buys it. It had been one of the most profitable lines in the West during Leadville's silver boom.

April 28, 1894 Strike-bound Cripple Creek is sending a contingent to join Coxey's Army. A. C. Fiske of the Pan-American Bi-Metallic Association calls on silver supporters to meet in Washington on May 22 to demand that silver "be restored to its ancient role, at a ratio not to exceed 16 to 1." The Sun prints the constitution of the newly formed Free Coinage Republican League of Pitkin County.

May 5, 1894 The Sun notes Coxey has arrived in Washington. While continuing its reports of persons leaving

Aspen for new homes elsewhere, the Sun optimistically opines that some Aspen mines will soon be working again.

May 19, 1894 Would-be members of Coxey's army commandeer a Union Pacific train in Montpelier, Idaho, to join Coxey in Washington. Police arrest them when the train arrives in Rock Springs, Wyoming. Noting that some Eastern papers are worrying about the drop in the $100 million gold reserve fund, the Sun says: "let them worry!"

May 26, 1894 In Washington, "General" Coxey is fined and sentenced to 20 days in jail for displaying a banner and walking on the grass at the Capitol.

Early June, 1894 Governor Waite of the People's (Populist) Party calls out Aspen's Company C of the Colorado National Guard for service in strike-torn Cripple Creek. Aspen real estate broker A. P. Mackay offers to sell 15 properties at 1/3 value. Bi-metallists in England are pleased that Kansas and Texas Democrats rejected free coinage of silver; the Englanders call for a new effort at international agreement on silver.

June 15, 1894 Twenty two Aspen men agree to form a tennis club. Among the founding members are Porter Nelson, Herbert McNair, Samuel I. Hallett and Harold W. Clark. Members agree to pay $5 on demand as needed for construction of courts.

June 30, 1894 The Sun quotes the London Financial News as saying that if the US bases its money on silver, British trade with the US will vanish in a year. It says over 500 men are now working for daily wages in Aspen silver mines, and another 470 are working as mine lessees.

July 10, 1894 The Imperial Currency Commission ends a long meeting in Berlin without making any proposal for silver in the Germany currency system. Silver supporters argue that at current prices, many mines will close.

July 28, 1894 Aspen and Leadville will have a telephone connection "before the snow flies." Big Eastern investor J. B. Wheeler comes to Aspen to complete arrangements to reopen his bank, which closed in the crisis year of 1893.

August 18, 1894 The Sun acidly notes that since Treasury Secretary Carlisle started minting silver dollars again and letting the gold reserve dwindle, gold lunatics who used to adore him are denouncing him. The US Mint has turned out 50,000 new silver dollars, but still has 121 million ounces of silver on hand to meet future needs.

August 25, 1894 The war over Korea between Japan and China, both silver countries, makes Aspen think better days may be ahead for silver. The Smuggler Mine, turning a profit of $50,000 a month, is putting in a new ore concentrator, designed by manager Samuel Irving Hallett. Wheeler's Aspen Mining and Smelting Company leases its smelter to Charles W. Ellis.

September 1, 1894 The Sun warns readers to watch out for counterfeit silver dollars dated 1891. The low cost of silver in a dollar coin means big profit for counterfeiters.

September 8, 1894 Recalling Governor Waite's use of the National Guard to protect workers during the Cripple Creek strike, Colorado Populists renominate him for Governor. The Sun says W. Porter Nelson is leaving Aspen for Culpeper to bring back his family, who have been visiting there.

September 15, 1894 The Sun reports that some Eastern capitalists are in town seeking to make investments in silver. Previously billing itself as politically independent, the Sun now becomes an avowed Aspen mouthpiece for the People's Party.

September 17, 1894 Treasury Secretary Carlisle releases a statement to the United Press on Treasury actions regarding silver. He says Treasury holdings of silver coinage have fallen by $3 million.

October 6, 1894 The Sun says that several mines on Smuggler Mountain are consolidating. Demand continues for certain Aspen silver mining stocks, with Mollie Gibson shares now fetching over $1.50.

October 10, 1894 The Mint turns out its 1.8 millionth silver dollar since production of these started 3 months earlier. With silver at 63 5/8 cents an ounce, the metal in each coin costs just 49 cents. Mollie Gibson shares rise to $2.07 ½. Still far below the peak of almost $12 a share.

October 21, 1894 The New York Times says that some investors are talking of a "pre-election rise" in security markets. The reason: with the Republicans assured of victory in the forthcoming elections, investors trust the Republicans to restore confidence and expand business.

October 26, 1894 Porter Nelson sells more land in Culpeper County, Va. (deed book 26, page 298).

November 7, 1894 Popular disenchantment with Cleveland, and the economic crisis, cost the Democrats control of both houses of Congress in the off-year elections. The silver price is stuck at 63.5 cents. With anti-silver Cleveland repudiated, Mollie Gibson shares are now over $2 and Smuggler shares are worth $2.20. Perhaps these prices reflect false optimism for silver: California Republicans who endorsed silver were roundly defeated, as were Ohio Democrats supporting silver. Pitkin County gives majorities to all People's Party candidates.

November 14, 1894 The fall of the gold reserve to $100 million alarms Treasury Secretary Carlisle. In the past 12 months, $73.7 million in gold was exported from the US. Carlisle sells another $50 million of 10 year bonds to raise money to buy gold. The 5% rate of interest offered is generous for the time. The Treasury receives bids totaling $180 million, some offering to pay 17% over par. By early December, 1894, the gold reserve is back over $110 million.

December 1, 1894 A strong demand for rental houses in Aspen reflects more men working and recovery from the 1893 panic. The Sun notes that despite the low price of silver, the two railroads serving Aspen are hauling out about the same amount of ore as before. Several more concentrating plants are likely to be built in Aspen. Aspenites think local mines could supply all the silver China might need to pay the indemnity Japan is likely to seek from China. Silver stocks are still being bought by investors from the Eastern states. Smuggler shares are going for $2.45 per $5 par value share. Jerome B.

Wheeler's Aspen Mining and Smelting Company shares currently fetch the second highest price of any Aspen mining company: $2.25 per $10 par value share.

December 7, 1894 Andrew Carnegie writes a letter to the Governor of Mississippi. In it, Carnegie says that until the country decisively chooses money of the highest value (i. e. based on gold), foreigners won't invest in the United States.

December 8, 1894 The Sun headlines its comment on Cleveland's speech to the second session of the 53rd Congress: "Monometallic Monstrous Mouthings Mainly Mythological Muck." Aspen dealers in mining stocks protest the always needy city's efforts to get them to pay a $100 occupation tax. The Sun later replaces local stock quotes with those from Colorado Springs. Did local stock traders give up in Aspen?

December 22, 1894 With a headline "Bow Before Britannia," the Sun claims that England is buying 300 to 350 thousand ounces of silver a month in the US for resale in countries where, unlike the US, silver is a store of value and not a commodity. It quotes Edwin Artel as saying "we are now practically under the rule of Queen Victoria, and Grover Cleveland is Prime Minister." The Aspen Mining and Smelting Company employed an average of 61 men during 1894, and produced over 7,700 tons of silver/lead ore worth $261,000.

December 24, 1894 The Mollie Gibson mine pays a $50,000 Christmas dividend, equivalent to five cents a share.

January 12, 1895 The Sun quotes experts who think the silver price has hit bottom. Smuggler-Durant mine owner

David Hyman says if the silver price falls to 55 cents, he'll close the Smuggler mill and stop shipping low grade ore.

January 24, 1895 The gold reserve falls below $70 million. The Sun takes out after its favorite target, President Grover Cleveland: "No use, Grover. You'll have to come to the silver medicine." It says that in Denver, one can hardly walk a block without being accosted by an indigent, and boasts that street begging is unknown in silver-lined Aspen.

January 28, 1895 President Cleveland asks Congress for permission to sell, directly to the public, small denomination long-term bonds redeemable in gold, and also to cancel Greenbacks and Sherman Act notes as fast as these could be bought up. The Springer bill incorporates these proposals. Silver interests oppose the bill, saying that the Treasury instead should just begin paying its obligations in silver.

January 31, 1895 The Treasury's gold reserve falls to $45 million, well below the $100 million target and a record low.

February 7, 1895 The House rejects the Springer bill, forcing Cleveland to turn again to a syndicate led by J. P. Morgan. The syndicate agrees to furnish 3.5 million ounces of gold, half to come from Europe, in exchange for $65 million in 4% bonds for which it will pay a premium of 4.5%. The syndicate sells the bonds at a premium of 12 1/4%. Opponents charge the Treasury with selling the bonds too cheaply, and the syndicate with profiteering. The Sun snootily comments: "Cleveland will probably go into the banking business after the country dispenses with his valuable service."

February 16, 1895 The Sun intemperately terms Cleveland's sale of bonds "thievery by an arch traitor." Silver boosters discover an 1857 law, never repealed, providing for the Treasury to accept Mexican coins in payment of debt, at the ratio of 20 cents US per Mexican quarter dollar. Silverites urge that US silver bullion be shipped to Mexico for coining, with the resulting Mexican coins then brought back for use in paying debts to the Treasury.

March 2, 1895 The Sun says German discussion of a new international monetary conference is boosting the silver price. It notes that several smelter representatives are in Aspen to drum up business. Among these is future Senator Simon Guggenheim (whose family owns the Philadelphia Smelter in Pueblo, forerunner of the giant American Smelting and Refining Company).

March 30, 1895 The silver price rises in New York by two cents an ounce, for a total one month's rise of 6 1/4 cents. Experts ascribe the improved price to Japanese acceptance of the Chinese armistice offer, and expectations for a large indemnity in silver to be paid by the latter. Also mentioned is renewed talk in Europe of bi-metallism in the world's currencies. Nonetheless, US silver exports since January 1 total only $7.5 million, versus $9.8 million in the first three months of 1894.

May 4, 1895 The Sun again attacks Cleveland, calling his letter to the Governor of Mississippi a "rehash of sound money platitudes," and an "exhibit of his feeble intellect." At current market prices, it takes 32 ounces of silver to buy one ounce of gold; silver forces still want free coinage of silver at the ratio of 16 to one! Cotton is going for as low as 4 7/8 cents a pound in New York. Several Aspen mines raise miners' wages from $2.25 to $2.50 a day. In the Aspen municipal elections, two parties are putting up candidates: the Citizen's Silver Party, and the People's Party.

May 11, 1895 The profitable Smuggler Mine increases its work force to 125 men, and resumes taking out low grade ore. Recovery from the 1893 Panic continues.

May 18, 1895 The Sun sees possible help coming from abroad: Chile will spend $10 million of its nitrate revenues to buy silver and will accept silver in exchange for gold. Also Australia declares its support for a new international monetary conference. The Sun still has nothing good to say about the Cleveland Administration. It comments on Treasury Secretary Carlisle's assertion that he would have to vote Republican if the national Democratic convention supports free coinage of silver. The Sun says Carlisle should "buy a cheap rope and hang himself." Many Aspen houses are for rent; example, a 6-room house on Lake Avenue is offered at $8 a month. What would that cost today?

May 26, 1895 The Sun praises the speech of the "eloquent young Nebraska Congressman" who addressed the Sound Money Convention in Memphis on May 21. Silver is 67 cents an ounce in New York.

June 8, 1895 In an editorial, the Sun denounces the idea that the US should await European approval to coin silver; it says international bi-metallism is a "deluxe" dream. Rep. Richard Bland, the power behind the Bland-Allison Act, comes to Aspen to pep up the troops. Aspen businesses advertise "free silver" prices, or "16 to 1" prices. Smuggler shares at $1.85 are the highest priced of Aspen mining stocks; Aspen Mining and Smelting is at $1.50, and Mollie Gibson at $0.98. The Aspen mine is shipping 1,200 tons of ore a month.

June 14, 1895 The Director of the US Mint issues his estimates of world production of precious metals in 1894. He puts world gold production of gold at 8.8 million ounces worth $181.5 million vs. an output valued at $158.8 in 1893. The figures for silver are 165.9 million ounces (worth $105 million at the average price for the year of 63 1/4 cents per ounce). The US is the largest producer of silver in 1894, with Mexico a close second. The US is the third largest producer of gold, after Australasia and Africa.

July 6, 1895 Spain expresses interest in taking part in the next international monetary conference. Spain has a bi-metallic monetary system based on a fixed ratio between silver and gold. Also, Spanish colonies such as Puerto Rico and the Philippines, are almost entirely on silver.

July 13, 1895 A Sun editorial waxes poetic: A resolute United States should stand tall, holding a yellow metal in one hand and a white metal in the other, between on one side a small white man (Europe) holding yellow metal, and on the other, a small yellow man (Asia) holding white metal.

Early August, 1895 Democrats favoring the free coinage of silver meet in Washington. The Sun notes the return of Porter Nelson to Aspen on the August 2 Rio Grande train.

August 24, 1895 The Connaughton Ranch, across the Roaring Fork River from Aspen, with potentially valuable mineral rights, is for sale at $3,700, with terms offered. It includes 172 acres and a six room, brick house with plaster walls. Not really a fire sale; owner Aspen pioneer Michael Connaughton is joining the flight from Aspen to Cripple Creek. He will die there six months later in a pneumonia epidemic. New outside investors buy the idle Holden Works for $2,600.

September 14, 1895 The Treasury gold reserve, at $96.3 million, is again below the $100 million target, dropping by more than $1 million in a day. J. P. Morgan announces that his syndicate will aid the government again and is amassing gold for this purpose. The Sun says one out of every 10 Aspen residents now owns a bicycle.

October 12, 1895 The Sun lists many Pitkin County properties to be sold on October 14 for nonpayment of county taxes. Porter Nelson owns two of these, both in Aspen and valued at $3170 and $1475 respectively. A realtor offers "to give away" for $80, a house and lot in Aspen. Have property values dropped so much? The Rio Grande railroad suspends its "laundry" trains to Glenwood Springs for the season. Aspenites will now have to wait until next year to take a train to go swimming in the Glenwood hot pool.

November 4, 1895 Julia Henry Nelson shares the platform with Mrs. D. R. C. Brown at the Monday Club. Mrs. Brown's topic is "Emerson;" Julia speaks on current affairs.

November 9, 1895 Smelters next year are expected to raise their charges for treating ore. The greatest increase, $3 a ton, will be for processing third grade ore, of which Aspen has a lot. The Argentium-Juniata mine passes its dividend.

<u>November 16, 1895</u> After four years of minting very few coins, Russia plans to issue 100 million gold rubles and 25 million silver rubles in 1896. Russian help for Aspen silver?

<u>End of November, 1895</u> The <u>Sun</u> reports that the number of miners in El Paso County (which includes Cripple Creek) has gone from 523 in 1893 to 4,300 now. It claims that a half dozen Cripple Creek mines are producing gold at a cost of 50 cents an ounce. Not fair, says the <u>Sun</u>; the US values gold at over $20 an ounce! Still, the paper denounces as completely false a Denver newspaper story to the effect that most of Aspen is moving to Cripple Creek.

<u>December 8, 1895</u> The <u>Sun</u> reports on Cleveland's message to the reassembled lame-duck Congress under the headline "Grover's Garrulity." It repeats without comment the portion of Cleveland's address saying that "no government and no act of legislation has ever been able to hold two metals together in a free coinage ratio appreciably different from that which is estimated in markets of the world." It also reports the return of Porter Nelson to Aspen, "somewhat improved in health," following several weeks' stay in Denver. The paper quotes Nelson as saying, after visiting Cripple Creek, that the latter promises to be the greatest mining camp the world has ever seen. But Cripple Creek is no place for a poor man. Accommodations are scarce, and many men must sleep on tables in saloons. Nelson says estimates of a Cripple Creek population of 75,000 by spring may be low. Is he thinking, like so many other Aspenites, of moving to Cripple Creek?

December 10, 1895 The Atchison, Topeka and Santa Fe Railroad goes through bankruptcy court, and abandons control of the bankrupt Colorado Midland Railroad which serves Aspen. The Midland will, however, operate until 1918.

December 14, 1895 The failure of the six Populist Senators to obstruct the organization of the Senate by the Republicans leads to speculation that they were bought off by a promise to reorganize the Senate Finance Committee in a way to favor silver. J. W. Deane, who filed the Aspen town site patent application in 1881 as a Pitkin County judge, moves from Aspen to Cripple Creek, and begins investing there.

December 20, 1895 Cleveland asks Congress for legislation to help float, on a more constructive basis, a new loan to buy gold. The silverites oppose. The next day, the Sun takes out after the President, printing an open letter "to G. Cleveland" beginning as follows: "Accept our humble admiration. You are the greatest fraud, the most magnificent harlequin, the biggest man of preposterous dignity and cold-blooded villainy our glorious county has ever produced."

December 28, 1895 The Sun says that in 1893, to "avoid entanglement with Europe," Cleveland rejected a Russian offer to lend the United States $60 million in gold for three years. Later, the paper terms Russia "our loyal gold friend."

January 4, 1896 Banker J. P. Morgan writes to President Cleveland offering to buy up to $200 million in bonds on the same terms as in 1895. He offers to pay in gold coin, and take steps to prevent gold exports from the US. Cleveland and Treasury Secretary Carlisle then decide to sell the bonds, not by private negotiation with a syndicate, but by public subscription. The Treasury invites the public to subscribe for $100 million. Bids opened February 5 total over $568 million, most at 112% to 114% of par. No need for a syndicate. By month's end, the gold reserve, which had fallen as low as $44.5 million, is back over $128 million.

January 11, 1896 The Sun discusses developments in the Crystal (Rock Creek) mining district, located in Gunnison County over the Elk Mountains from Aspen. Hayden's survey parties had noted good mineral prospects there. Porter Nelson, President of the Bear Mountain Mining Company, returns to Aspen after two weeks in Crystal where he had let a contract for the construction of a 600-foot tunnel to develop company properties encompassing 27 different claims. Nelson brings 50 pounds of ore samples to Aspen for testing. Some shipments of Bear Mountain ore have averaged 92 ounces of silver per ton, with traces of gold. That is rich ore.

January 22, 1896 In the eyes of many, Republican Senator Teller of Colorado is likely to become head of a proposed Free Silver Party. Henry Cowenhoven, an Aspen pioneer and probably its richest citizen, dies suddenly. He started by selling supplies to miners and then invested in mines.

February 1, 1896 The Senate passes a free coinage of silver bill by 48 to 41, with 24 Democrats supporting and only 15 against. As states pick delegates to the forthcoming Democratic convention, silverites capture many seats. The Sun editorializes that "the gold organs of the East are becoming frantic in their efforts to prevent an alliance between the Populists and pro-silver forces from outside the Populists."

February 15, 1896 Despite the support of House Speaker Crisp, the House votes down a pro-silver amendment to the bill authorizing the issuance of bonds to buy gold. The Sun lists Mrs. W. Porter Nelson as one of many guests at a "magnificent" ball given by Mr. and Mrs. S. I. Hallett at the Hotel Jerome. Julia Henry goes alone because Porter is away looking at gold properties in the Cripple Creek area. Samuel I. Hallett, manager of David Hyman's mining properties in Aspen, is from New York. Julia Henry's great great grandmother was from the Hallett family that in the 17th century settled in what is now Astoria, New York. Are Julia Henry and Samuel I. Hallett distant cousins?

February 16, 1896 In a letter to Porter in Cripple Creek, Julia Henry shows some annoyance at being stranded with the children and a cook who is threatening to quit: "Your last two letters which say first that you expect to be in Cripple Creek most of the time and then that you wouldn't be home until March first made me mad and dismayed me. You must think that I am very meek or fond of staying alone, I don't know which. . . . I heard of several girls this week but they were principally those Swedes. . . . I think it would be better to let Annie go when her month is up." Julia is appeased the next day by a letter from Porter promising an early return, and sending her a new supply of calling cards. Can't be without those in Aspen society.

February 29, 1896 Morale is important. The Sun writes: "Aspen is all right . . . but it would be a relief to the people of Aspen if the croaker who is continually publishing his woes would go to Hallam Lake and tell his troubles to the fishes."

March 7, 1896 The Sun goes after Cleveland again under the caption "Grover's Piety: Now comes Grover Cleveland posing as President of the Home Missionary Society of New York. And he tells the Christians of that pious city to send missionaries out to enlighten the benighted people of those states away out on the frontier . . . But what does Grover Cleveland know about Colorado and the West, anyhow? Away with such cant and hypocrisy." On the local scene, the Sun says some mines in Crystal and vicinity contain enough silver, lead and copper to cover completely all development costs, as well as much gold from which good dividends come.

March 14, 1896 The Belgian Prime Minister states in Parliament that Belgium will go along with any international agreement to fix a ratio between silver and gold.

March 21, 1896 Under Mayor Hooper of the Peoples Party, Aspen sets its 1896 budget at $35,000, and slashes employee salaries. Quite a drop from the peak budget of $60,000 set in 1891 under Republican B. Clark Wheeler.

March 28, 1896 Excitement among stock traders; rumors of rich strikes in Aspen float about. In one day, Gibson stock opens at 72 cents, jumps to 84 cents, closes at 79 cents.

April 4, 1896 US mints are turning out silver dollars at the rate of 1.5 million coins a month, using silver bullion the Treasury bought under the Sherman Act. Plans are announced for the construction of a telephone line between Aspen and Glenwood Springs.

April 18, 1896 Results of the Aspen municipal elections show the Populists winning all vacant seats. Aspen hears more rumors of rich strikes in the Crystal mining district.

May 8, 1896 Julia Henry writes to Porter, still away from Aspen despite a promised early return: "Stallard told me this morning that you had written him to forward your mail to Box 1384, Cripple Creek, so I am going to send this letter there & hope it will reach you before you leave for Denver. I sent my last to Victor, % Joe Remy, but haven't known where it went then. I do hope you are coming home soon, the children are asking when Father is coming back." Edgar Stallard is from Culpeper Virginia, and has offices in Nelson's Aspen block. Julia's letters show she is not pining at home: Example: "I have just returned from a Kensington tea at Mrs. Lysters. I am going to write a little letter before supper as I am going the Guthrie's afterwards." Again: "Mrs. Clark and Bert Gillespie called Monday night and I invited them and Harold to supper last night. So with entertaining the Magazine Club at 2 PM, I was rushed all day. Carmer and Kate stayed up to supper; I wish you could see how beautifully they behaved. This afternoon I go to a Kensington tea at the Kitchens and to a progressive diner at Lysters tonight. Annie (the cook) is furious as she won't get to church tonight."

May 23, 1896 The Sun says that Crystal mines like the Black Eagle, Lead King and Lucky Boy, in which Aspen investors have ownership shares, are doing well.

End May, 1896 Senator Teller gives the press more information about how the Sherman Silver Purchase Act came about. Teller says that Silver Republicans in the Senate were determined to attach a free silver rider to the McKinley Tariff bill. This would have led to a veto by President Harrison, meaning that neither the silverites nor the high tariff parties would have gotten anything. Anti-silver Republicans then decided to support the Sherman bill as a lesser evil than free coinage. A social note from the Sun: "the bloomer craze has hit Aspen, and almost everywhere ladies can be seen on the streets riding bicycles and wearing big-legged pants with the required hump. Who says we are not becoming metropolitan?"

June 6, 1896 The silver price rises toward 70 cents an ounce. The Sun says 2,000 men would go to work in Aspen at a price of 90 cents, and many who have gone to Cripple Creek would come back. It also quotes W. Porter Nelson, principal owner of the Bear Mountain properties in Crystal, as saying on his return to Aspen that several Crystal mine owners have bags of ore stacked awaiting opening of the new jack train road over the 10,700 foot high Schofield Pass to the railhead at Crested Butte. Nelson said the digging under contract of the tunnel at the Bear Mountain properties is proceeding well, and will reach the main ore body soon.

June 16, 1896 At the Virginia state convention, Democrats hiss at the mention of Cleveland's name. The Sun remarks that the silver tide is flooding south. Cleveland gives a statement to the New York Herald saying that he refuses to believe that the national Democratic Party at its convention would be so unpatriotic or foolish as to call for free and unlimited coinage of silver. The Sun goes after Treasury Secretary Carlisle in an editorial: "It should surprise no one that Carlisle's speeches are being sent through the mail at government expense. The Cleveland Administration is marked by petty pilfering as well as grand larceny." In Aspen, the Post Office moves to its new building.

June 25, 1896 The Acting Secretary of the Interior concurs in the recommendation of the Commissioner of the General Land Office that the Department of Justice sue to correct errors in the Aspen town site patent, no. 647 in the Leadville, Colorado series.

June 27, 1896 The Sun dislikes Treasury Secretary Carlisle about as much as President Cleveland. It sneers that if Cleveland and Carlisle go into law in New York when they leave government, they can hang out a sign saying: "We have robbed the American people successfully. Surely we can be of assistance to you."

June 27, 1896 American cereal, cotton and tobacco farmers received $729 million less for the harvest of 1895 than for the harvest of 1891. American stock raisers received $734 million less in 1895 than in 1891. Blaming all this on silver demonetization, the Sun opines: "the farmer or any other producer who votes against a free silver candidate ought to be harnessed upon alongside a donkey; but that would be rather hard on the donkey to force upon him such a stupid mate."

Political conventions, 1896: The Republicans hold their convention in Saint Louis in June. They name William McKinley of Ohio as their candidate for President. The convention votes down a plank submitted by a minority led by Senator Henry Teller of Colorado calling for unlimited coinage of silver at a 16:1 ratio. Twenty-three Republicans then follow Teller out of the hall. The convention approves a platform plank saying that the Republican Party is "unreservedly for sound money. It caused the enactment of a law providing for the redemption [resumption] of specie payments in 1879. Since then every dollar has been as good as gold. We are unalterably opposed to every measure calculated to debase our currency or to impair the credit of our country. We are therefore opposed to the free coinage of silver except by international agreement . . ."

The Democrats open their convention in Chicago in July. Among the delegates is Samuel I. Hallett, Aspen's leading mining engineer. The Party names William Jennings Bryan of Nebraska as its Presidential candidate, electrified by his oratory against "crucifying mankind on a cross of gold." Silver forces show their strength by rejecting the National Committee's choice of Governor Hill of anti-silver New York as temporary chairman and instead elect Senator John W. Daniel of pro-silver Virginia. Senator Jones reads a platform plank attacking Cleveland's issuance of bonds to buy gold as "trafficking with syndicates." In repudiating Cleveland, the Democratic platform is even more fervent against gold mono-metallism. It calls "the money question paramount to all others at this time . . . We are unalterably opposed to mono-metallism which has locked fast the prosperity of an industrial people in the paralysis of hard times. Gold mono-metallism is a British policy, and its adoption has brought other nations into financial servitude to London . . . We demand the free and unlimited coinage of both gold and silver at the present legal ratio of 16 to 1 without waiting for the aid or consent of any other nation. We demand that the standard silver dollar be a full legal tender, equally with gold, for all debts, public and private." The platform is adopted by 608 votes to 301. Cleveland's Navy Secretary announces he will not support the

Democratic platform adopted in Chicago. The Sun comments: "These Cleveland cuckoos are not so thoroughly sick of democracy as to give up their jobs."

In Saint Louis in July, the People's Party also endorses William Jennings Bryan as its Presidential candidate. In Aspen, business comes to a halt as people cheer this news.

July 11-18, 1896 Brokers expect the shares of Aspen mines such as the Mollie Gibson and Argentium-Juniata to rise following adoption of the pro-silver Democratic platform. The output of the major mines around Aspen in 1895, as listed for tax purposes, is (in dollars):

Della S.	444,660
Aspen Mining Co.	247,199
Aspen Mining and Smelting	172,268
Argentium-Juniata	158,164
Mollie Gibson	138,965
Durant	74,710
Smuggler	67,790

A lot in the Hallam addition to Aspen sells for $200. The Sun goes after Cleveland again: "Information has gone forth that Grover the great will soon give a letter to the press of the country, the import of which will be criticism of the Chicago convention. It will be distributed over the John Hancock of his royal fatness, Grover Cleveland."

July 21, 1896 Secretary of Interior Hoke Smith writes to the Attorney General asking the Department of Justice to take steps to cancel Aspen's original town site patent, or to reform it. Smith advises that the Aspen town fathers will not oppose such actions. Attorney General Judson Harmon replies 3 days later, saying it is not only within Interior's power, but indeed is Interior's duty, to correct the problem.

July 25, 1896 The Sun reports that Crystal's Lead King mine is producing ore with 200 ounces of metal a ton, 40% to 60% lead and 35% copper.

August 6, 1896 The First Assistant Attorney of the Department of Interior bucks to the Commissioner of the General Land Office, the Attorney General's July 24 letter on the Aspen town site "for such action as the Land Office deems appropriate." The Land Office sends Aspen a letter 20 days later asking that the original town site patent be returned to it for cancellation.

August 7, 1896 Democrats opposed to the Chicago Democratic platform meet in Indianapolis. The Sun reports that more work is going on in the Crystal mining district than ever before at this time of year. Most work is to meet the annual assessment requirements of the 1872 mining law, but some operators hope to ship ore later in the summer.

August 15, 1896 The Sun says that W. Porter Nelson and J. F. MacMillan, President of the Aspen Favorite Mining Company, inspected that company's properties. Based on a test showing over 60 ounces of silver a ton, they decide not to lease out the company's mine in the Maroon district (now a wilderness area). Instead, the company itself hires men to work the mine.

August 22, 1896 The Lead King mine in Crystal produces the largest galena nugget ever seen in Gunnison County, 1800 pounds of almost 100% pure galena. Porter Nelson later will become owner of the Lead King mine.

August 29, 1896 The Sun says that James G. Blaine's prediction is coming to pass: the white man with yellow metal in his hand is at a severe disadvantage facing the yellow man with white metal in his hand. Reports of large Japanese subsidies for ships trading with the US prompt this comment.

September 5, 1896 The long strike in Leadville may be ending. With water rising in the mines, one operator plans to hire union miners and pay them the $3 a day they want. More good news from Crystal about the Lead King: the shaft is down only 20 feet, but already the mine has yielded five car loads of shippable ore.

September 12, 1896 Legal action by the Crystal River Land and Improvement Company blocks the foreclosure sale of the road bed of the Crystal River Railroad. Some Crystal mines are now shipping their ore out by mule over the 10,700 foot high Schofield Pass to the Denver Rio Grande railhead at Crested Butte.

September 21, 1896 The Aspen City Council discusses, and refers to its Ways and Means Committee, the request of the General Land Office that old town site patent be surrendered so that the Office can reissue a new patent showing the proper boundaries of Aspen. Mollie Gibson shares are quoted at 48 to 50 cents, Argentium-Juniata at 49.5 to 50 cents.

September 28, 1896 Aspen's Ways and Means Committee reports to the full City Council that it sees no objection to surrendering the original town site patent. Mineral rights under lot L, block 100 in Aspen sell for a nominal $1, plus unstated additional "valuable considerations."

October 17, 1896 The Sun hits out at, not this time at lame duck Cleveland, but at its new target: "Bill McKinley must find it fearfully monotonous receiving the homage of coerced hundreds who daily ride to Canton on forced excursions. But there is a consolation for the Hanna puppet - his show days will soon be over and he can return to private life." Grasping at any straw, the Sun points out that the coinage on demand provisions of the 1837 Mint Act (5 Stat. 136) are still in force. Section 14 of that Act provides that "gold and silver bullion brought to the mint for coinage shall be received and coined by the proper officials, for the benefit of the depositors."

October 26, 1896 The Aspen Favorite Mining Company holds a special stockholders meeting to discuss raising new capital to pay off its debt of $600 and patent its properties. The options: sell stock, or take out a mortgage. J. F. MacMillan is elected President, and Edgar Stallard, Secretary.

November 3, 1896 Big New York brokerage houses decide to stay open all night to accommodate customers wanting to dump US stocks in London if Bryan wins. But Republican McKinley handily defeats Bryan. The Republicans also keep control of both the House and Senate. Colorado, strongly pro-silver, goes Democratic. Meanwhile, as Aspen earlier overtook rival Leadville in mine output, so now Cripple Creek easily eclipses Aspen, turning out $20 million in gold vs. Aspen's $2 million in silver production.

STATE OF COLORADO

SS

COUNTY OF PITKIN

John McNeill being first duly sworn on oath says, That he is Mayor pro tem of the city of Aspen, Pitkin County, State of Colorado, acting in the place of the Mayor of said city now absent; that he has made and caused to be made, diligent search for the patent of the Aspen Townsite, issued for said townsite by the United states Government to J. W. Deane, County and Probate Judge in trust for the inhabitants of the Town of Aspen and to his successors in trust on theThird day of March A. D. 1885, and cannot find the same and cannot therefore surrender the same in compliance with Letter "N" of the Honorable Acting Commissioner of the General land Office of the date of August 26th, A. D. 1896.

Affiant therefore asks on behalf of said city that a corrected patent be issued for said Townsite in conformity with said Letter of the Honorable Acting Commissioner.

Sworn and subscribed to before me, this 30th, day of October A.D. 1896.

MY COMMISSION EXPIRES
NOVEMBER 9, 1898.

Mayor pro-tem McNeill swears that the original town site patent cannot be found, witnessed by City Attorney Clark

City Clerks' Office

Aspen, Colo., December 8,1896.

Register & Receiver,

U.S.Land Office,

Glenwood Springs,Colo.

At a regular meeting of the City Council of Aspen, held on April 20th,1896. John McNeill was nominated by the said City Council for Mayor Pro tem, a ballot was taken which resulted in the unanimous election of the said John McNeill,Mayor Protem for the fiscal year ending on the 18th day of April,1897.

He has,ever since said election,been acting as said Mayor Pro tem, in the absence of the Mayor.

I hereby certify that the foregoing is correct in every respect.

Given under my hand and the seal of said City of Aspen, this 8th day of December,A.D.1896.

J D Hooper
Mayor.

Attest,

Alice P. Grove
City Clerk.

Mayor Hooper and City Clerk Grover confirm that John McNeill was Aspen Mayor pro-tem

November 7, 1896 Grasping at straws, the Sun says Bryan still has a chance, despite McKinley's election victory claims. It also reports that English bi-metallists interpret McKinley's win as a victory for international bi-metallism.

November 14, 1896 Silver is 64 3/4 cents an ounce, lead is $2.75 a hundredweight. Argentium-Juniata stock is 46 cents bid, 48 offered. Mollie Gibson is 55 cents bid, 55 3/4 offered. Not much price change after the election.

November 21, 1896 The Sun: "England helped fight the anti-silver forces in the last campaign with her influence and money, even when she knew that the alternative was McKinley with a Chinese wall of protectionism. Isn't it ludicrous now to hear the Administration talk about raising the club of protectionism to force John Bull to accept bi-metallism?"

November 28, 1896 The Sun hasn't forgotten Grover: "Grover Cleveland was bold enough to set the pace and inaugurate a system of finances which will enslave the peoples of this nation for all time, and his successors will likely have the courage to continue it."

December 5, 1896 Several Aspen miners who earlier went to the latest hot mining camp, Kootenay, British Columbia, send back encouraging reports. David Hyman of Cincinnati, one of the big investors in Aspen, returns from checking out Kootenay. Angus McPherson, a pioneer grocer in Aspen, goes bankrupt, as does the Weinberg Clothing Store.

December 19, 1896 The Kootenay craze is dying out, but now some half dozen discouraged Aspenites are turning their eyes to greener (really more golden?) pastures in South America. Aspen businessmen form a Chamber of Commerce to try to persuade railroads to reduce ore shipping charges.

December 31, 1896 Senator Edward Wolcott of Colorado and General Francis A. Walker of Massachusetts are going abroad, with McKinley's blessing, to sound out European bimetallists on prospects for an international agreement on silver's role in world monetary systems.

CHAPTER EIGHT

KEEPING HOPE ALIVE

Early, 1897 Aspen's active miners are fewer than 1,500 at the start of 1897, down from 2,300 in 1895. Of these, about 600 are working for daily wages and the remainder are operating mines for themselves as lessees. Silver is priced at 64 3/4 cents an ounce, and lead at 2.90 cents a pound. The output of the major Aspen mines in the preceding year, measured in dollars, is estimated as follows:

Della S.	444,650
Aspen Mine, incl. North lease	275,000
Argentium-Juniata	175,150
Smuggler	163,900

January 9, 1897 The Sun keeps up its attacks on the lame duck President: "No matter what kind of President Mayor McKinley will be, people will be glad to have done with Grover Cleveland . . . only 60 more days!"

January 14, 1897 The Commissioner of the General Land Office in Washington informs the Land Office Recorder in Glenwood Springs that the Aspen town site patent, no. 647 of the Leadville series issued March 3, 1847, has been revoked by the agreement with the Aspen city authorities, and that a new patent will be issued. It is, 15 days later, Patent Volume (Misc.) 12, page 192, Leadville series.

January 30, 1897 Aspen's surviving millionaire, David Robinson Crockett Brown, resigns as Vice President of the First National Bank. He is moving most of his activities elsewhere (years later he comes back to Aspen banking with the Aspen State Bank). The owners of the Bonnybelle, Park Regent, Bushwhacker and Pride of Aspen mines agree to cut the royalties they charge lessees for ore assaying 60 ounces of silver a ton or less. Aspen businessmen want railroads to lower freight charges, and smelters to lower refining charges, to keep more Aspen mines working. A Chamber of Commerce delegation will go Denver to put the plan to the railroads.

February 13, 1897 The Aspen Chamber of Commerce decides to promote business with cities such as New Orleans and Galveston, in retaliation against New York, St. Louis and Chicago, now dominant in Western wholesale trade. The latter cities voted solidly against pro-silver Bryan.

February 27, 1897 In Washington, the House by a 297 to three vote passes a bill endorsing the idea of a new international monetary conference which could help restore silver's luster. With Cleveland soon to leave office, the Sun finds a new target: "The Cabinet which Mr. McKinley is assembling about him can be characterized as the infirmary, because to date the material in its constitution is worm eaten and weakened by dry rot. . . . There is no young blood in the McKinley Cabinet. Corrupt beggars and waivers of the bloody shirt will counsel and advise the Canton mayor how to conduct the affairs of this glorious republic."

March 6, 1897 Mayor Hooper, who had been forced by ill health to leave Aspen for a lower altitude, returns to preside over a City Council meeting. The Sun notes Congress's nullification of a Cleveland Executive Order placing 21 million acres of national forests in Colorado, Wyoming, Utah, Montana, South Dakota, Idaho and Washington off limits to claiming under the various land acts: "For a man whose knowledge of the country is confined to a few duck marshes and fishing holes along the Atlantic Coast, this proclamation (Cleveland's Order) was a high-handed procedure."

March 13, 1897 The Sun says Crystal will be a booming camp this summer. A smelter is to be built there in the spring, and investors from Illinois and Colorado may put in an electric power station.

March 20, 1897 At the Brown Palace hotel in Denver, Senator Teller presides over a meeting to select a delegation to the national convention of Silver Republicans. In Crystal, work is almost complete on deepening the shaft of the Lead King mine to 100 feet. Representatives of the Hoffman Smelting and Refining Company, which plans to build a smelter at Marble to serve the Crystal mines, are in St. Louis to buy machinery. The machinery will be shipped to Marble when the roads are open. In Aspen, County Commissioner Vince Johnson is scaring up Democratic voters and candidates for the April municipal elections.

March 30-April 4, 1897 Aspen City Clerk Alice B. Grover certifies the list of candidates nominated by the three Aspen parties - Peoples, Democratic and Silver Republican - for the April 6 municipal election. The Sun warns that a vote against People's Party candidates in Aspen's election means a vote to pay the water company for putting up a dozen unneeded hydrants. It says that in the case of the People's Party candidates in the coming election, "the office sought the man." The Sun here refers, among others, to political neophyte W. Porter Nelson. Nelson is a surprise choice as the People's

Party mayoral nominee. His opponents are Democrat R. G. Withers and Republican L. R. Tucker. Nelson is shown as living at 205 (should be 215) West Hallam Street and as having offices in the Aspen Block, 303 S. Galena.

List of Nominations.

Notice is hereby given that the following is a list of nominations certified to the city clerk of Aspen, Colo., to be voted for at the city election to be held Tuesday, April 6, 1897:

FOR MAYOR.	
W. PORTER NELSON. 205 W. Hallam St. and Aspen block.	People's Party.
ROBERT G. WITHERS. 412 W. Francis St. and Keene block.	Democratic Party.
L. R. TUCKER. [illegible] East Hyman avenue.	National Silver and Silver Republican
FOR CITY ENGINEER.	
GEORGE W. NYCE. 315 West Hallam, St. and Aspen block.	People's Party and Silver Republican
FOR CITY TREASURER.	
FANNY BOND. 941 East Cooper avenue and City Hall.	People's, National Silver and Silver Republican
HATTIE M. HERRICK. 111 East Cooper avenue.	Democratic [illegible]
FOR ALDERMAN, First Ward, (long term.)	
SIM C. McNEILL. [illegible] Durant street.	People's Party.
JACOB SANDS. [illegible] East Hopkins Av. and 128 E. Hyman Av.	Democratic National Silver and Silver Republican Parties.

FOR ALDERMAN First Ward, (short term.)	
EUGENE COLE. 829 East Hyman avenue.	People's Party.
J. B. PUTNAM. 616 East Cooper avenue.	National Silver and Silver Republican Parties.
JOSEPH R. JOHNS. 915 East Hyman avenue.	Democratic Party.
FOR ALDERMAN Second Ward.	
ED THEMER. Jerome Stables, 116 North Mill Street.	People's Party.
JOHN R. MASON. 320-322 East Hopkins.	Democratic Party.
CHARLES L. MOORE. 520 East Main street and Della S. mine.	Silver Republican and National Silver Parties.
FOR ALDERMAN Third Ward.	
A. D. BOURQUIN. 701 West Main street.	People's Party.
THEODORE G. LYSTER. 135 W. Smuggler St. and First National Bank	Democratic Party.
HENRY BECK. 113 E. Hopkins Av. and 535 E. Cooper Av.	Silver Republican and National Silver Parties.

Given under my hand and seal this 30th day of March, A. D. 1897.
[SEAL.] ALICE B. GROVER, City Clerk.

Candidate list for Aspen election, April, 1897

<u>April 7, 1897</u> Returns show that People's Party candidates win all the seats at stake in Aspen's April 6 election. Nelson is the weakest of the Party's candidates, carrying only four

of Aspen's nine precincts. Still, he out polls runner-up Republican Tucker by 77 votes.

April 17, 1897 The Sun opines that silver is not dead, pointing to results of local elections in Midwestern states that had supported Harrison earlier. It predicts that if Bryan is alive in 1900, he will be elected President. Mollie Gibson shares drop rapidly towards 10 cents a share, on rumors of an assessment of share owners, and/or lack of paying ore.

April 23, 1897 Porter Nelson assumes office as Mayor of Aspen, vice retiring People's Party Mayor Hooper. He names himself Chairman of the City Council's Health Committee, but takes no seat on any of the other nine Committees. Nelson now must be in Aspen every Monday night for the weekly Council meeting. If Nelson is ever absent, Alderman Fred Stockman will be Mayor pro tem, just as Alderman McNeill had been Mayor pro tem for Hooper.

May 1, 1897 The Sun says that Aspenites continue to flock to the Red River mining camp in New Mexico. Railroads advertise a fare of $20.20 from Aspen to Red River City.

May 7, 1897 A Washington despatch says that Colorado Republican Senator Edward G. Wolcott is sailing for Europe to explore prospects for international bi-metallism.

May 8, 1897 Jerome B. Wheeler's two banks, one in Aspen and one in Manitou, close for the second time. The Aspen bank turns over to Herbert L. McNair, trustee for the creditors, stock in many Aspen mining properties (but none in the Aspen Mining and Smelting Company). Wheeler's

Aspen bank may have sought bankruptcy protection, but his Aspen Mining and Smelting Company buys at a Sheriff's sale all the Porphyry Mountain and Richmond Hill properties of J. W. Deane. Deane, now active in mining elsewhere, helped B. Clark Wheeler secure the original Aspen town site patent.

<u>May 17, 1897</u> The Denver Rio Grande and the Midland Railroads turn down the request of the Aspen Chamber of Commerce for lower freight rates on low grade ore, and for a rate reduction on all ore orginating in outlying places like Ashcroft. The railroads say that 70% of shipments from Aspen are of low grade ore (below 25 ounces of silver a ton). The railroads, with heavy fixed costs to meet, are themselves hurting badly from traffic decreases.

<u>June 5, 1897</u> Prompted by Mayor Nelson, the Aspen City Council adopts a surprise resolution instructing the City Marshall to enforce the anti-gambling laws. This is not the first attempt to get tough on sin in Aspen.

<u>June 12, 1897</u> At Mayor Nelson's suggestion, the Aspen City Council instructs the City Attorney to draw up an ordinance levying a $300 license fee on drug store owners, and banning them from selling liquor by the drink. Silver is 59 7/8 cents an ounce, lead is 3 1/8 cents a pound.

<u>June 19, 1897</u> T. J. Monaghan, a socially prominent Aspenite and owner of the Buckhorn Saloon, is fined $20 for keeping his establishment open beyond closing hours. At the Aspen armory, Mayor Nelson welcomes teachers coming to town for a meeting of the Teachers Normal Institute for the 13th District. In Crystal, several mines, including the Lead

King, are now shipping out ore by wagon to the Carbondale railhead. The Crystal Valley Railroad is expected to reach Leggets (Redstone) soon, and work is progressing on the smelter at Marble. Aspen is keeping an eye on Crystal.

June 26, 1897 The Sun reports that Porter Nelson is in Crystal to look after his mining interests there. It charges rival Aspen Times with distributing false information about the Buckhorn Saloon case. Aspen names its delegates to a gold congress in Denver in July, and to the Trans-Mississippi Congress in Salt Lake City.

July 3, 1897 Aspenites are alarmed and distressed by the action of the state Game Warden in charging the operators of the Smuggler ore concentrator with polluting the Roaring Fork by dumping tailings into the river. The plant treats ores not only from the Smuggler Mine, but also from the Free Silver, the Argentium-Juniata, and Mollie Gibson mines. Closing the plant could jeopardize the jobs of hundreds of Aspenites.

July 10, 1897 Are things so bad? The Sun says more ore is being shipped out of Aspen than at any time in the past two years. A party from Aspen goes over Maroon Pass to Crystal to see about developing mines there. The City Council finally passes the ordinance proposed by Mayor Nelson regulating and taxing drug store owners, but cuts the tax rate in half to $100 for six months. The Sun terms the Wolcott mission to Europe a Republican dodge in advance of forthcoming off-year elections designed to deceive people into thinking that the GOP is a friend of silver.

July 17, 1897 Samuel I. Hallett, local manager of David Hyman's Smuggler and Durant mines, says that to cut pollution, his company will henceforth impound tailing water. Mayor Nelson, who had taken on the task of finding the right man to be Aspen dog catcher, asks the Council for more time, which is granted. Several Aspenites order new machinery to restart an inactive ore concentrator at Schofield, a few miles up from Crystal on the trail across Schofield Pass to the Denver and Rio Grande railhead at Crested Butte.

July 24, 1897 At the Trans-Mississippi Convention in Salt Lake City, W. J. Bryan makes an eloquent speech for silver. A motion there to endorse gold mono-metallism receives only five votes, all from Missouri. The Sun's comment: "When a Missourian goes to a convention of any sort, he invariably takes with him his unquenchable thirst . . . They raise good hogs in Missouri, but that's all." Klondike fever hits Aspen. Among those deciding to move to the gold fields in Alaska is People's Party Alderman Gus Bourquin.

July 31, 1897 A number of Aspenites are planning to head for the Klondike, the Sun says, to raise money to pay their Pitkin County taxes. The Sun comments: since dogs sell for $3 a pound in Alaska, "there are ample opportunities for enterprising Aspenites." Mayor Nelson tells the Council that he has appointed a man to be Aspen's dog tax collector, and has given him the rank of Deputy Marshall.

August 7, 1897 Silver is down to 55 ½ cents an ounce, the drop being ascribed to speculators. Aspen's Bushwhacker Mine suspends development work on its own. It will now give leases to miners who want to develop new areas. In a Pitkin

Court, Buckhorn owner Monaghan wins a suit against Aspen over the fine imposed on him for closing his saloon late.

August 14, 1897 A replacement is selected for Alderman Bourquin who left for the Klondike. At the suggestion of a visiting Post Office official, Mayor Nelson makes informal inquiries to see if Aspenites want home delivery service restored. He advises that there is no demand for such a service. With silver still below 56 cents, the Sun begins to talk up gold mining possibilities around Aspen.

August 17, 1897 The London Times says the Wolcott bi-metallic mission to Europe shows the "characteristic crudeness and boldness of American diplomacy." In Aspen, a major grocer fails and turns over his business to creditors. Mayor Nelson appoints Aspen delegates, not including himself, to the Western Slope Congress meeting at Delta in September.

August 21, 1897 Silver drops to 52 3/4 cents an ounce, while wheat goes above $1 a bushel. Will farmers continue to think that gold mono-metallism is so awful?

September 4, 1897 The Sun prints a letter written by former Alderman Bourquin on his way to the Klondike. This is the first of many such letters the paper will print from Aspenites seeking fortunes elsewhere. The paper again attacks the gold bugs: "The money fiends are now turning their batteries on Mexico, in an effort to force that country to abandon silver. They captured Germany, then the US, then France, then poor Japan, which country had to bow to them after an expensive war. Mexico has been, and is, prosperous beyond any other country (oh?), under the system of the free coinage of silver."

The latest scarlet fever epidemic in Aspen is dying out, as only two new cases are reported. Aspen's new dog catcher is doing well; the city treasury is now taking in considerable money from residents paying their dog taxes.

September 11, 1897 The railroads agree, at last, to reduce the freight rates from Aspen on low grade ore (under 30 ounces of silver per ton), so long as the silver price is below 57 cents. The Sun wonders if mine owners will now deliver on their promise to cut their royalties.

October 2, 1897 Reports are confirmed that the Bank of England will henceforth keep 1/5 of its monetary reserves in the form of silver coins issued in England. The Sun optimistically notes that at present prices, this action will immobilize 62 million ounces of silver. Two Aspenites return from Crystal over Maroon Pass in just five hours, reporting much activity in Crystal and a very good ore body at the Lead King mine. Aspen still keeps an eye on Crystal.

October 9, 1897 Silver rises to 58 cents on rumors of purchases for India. The City Council considers complaints about an incident where Mayor Nelson had the city stock policeman impound a certain lady's wandering cattle. Upon being released, these cattle made a nuisance of themselves in another resident's garden. The Council decides that the Mayor had made only one mistake, that of impounding the beasts in the first place. The Council instructs the Mayor and the Finance Committee to take action against the bondsman for the city treasurer in order to protect the city's interest in its money tied up by closure of the Wheeler bank.

November 18, 1897 The National Fire Prevention Company in Akron, Ohio writes to Mayor Nelson offering their services in putting out a stubborn fire in the Smuggler Mine. Since a local mine worker had just managed to bring the fire under control, the Mayor replies that the company is too late. Aspenites take pride in their own firefighting abilities.

November 20, 1897 City officials respond to new complaints of Aspen residents about loose stock in the city, saying that they will impound such animals during the winter just as they had done during the summer.

December 11, 1897 Coloradans take pride in the fact that uranium, hitherto considered a precious metal, is being mined in Gilpin County. Uranium is much sought abroad as a gun metal. Reporting that a new group of Aspen residents is about to set off for the Klondike, the Sun says that 99 out of a 100 who go there would do just as well prospecting in Colorado. It castigates a Denver paper for saying that Aspen will be emptied by people flocking to Alaska. To a report in a Victor, Colorado newspaper about a resident of Aspen returning from the Klondike with enough money to pay off his debts, the Sun demands rhetorically: "Show us such a man!" On the positive side, a British company based at Finsbury Circus, London, and operating under the name New Aspen Silver Mines, Ltd., buys some minor Aspen mines.

December 20, 1897 At the regular Monday meeting of the City Council, Mayor Nelson, City Attorney Clark and Alderman Stockman, previously appointed a special committee to look into the long dispute between the city and the Castle Creek Water Company over hydrants, report to the Council that they have persuaded the company to make what they consider a reasonable offer. In effect, the water company agrees to allow the city to use all 42 hydrants for the same $756 a quarter that the city had been paying for 36 hydrants. The Council approves this settlement. Mayor Nelson informs the Council that he has hired a new man to enforce the ordinance against loose stock.

January 1, 1898 The Sun takes issue with a recent statement by Treasury Secretary Gage claiming that gold has been the standard of value in the United States for 60 years. The silver price is 57 cents an ounce, lead is 3.60 cents a pound.

January 22, 1898 Plans are being drawn up to convert the idle Holden works into a concentrator to serve mines on West Aspen mountain. Could Aspen be coming back?

January 29, 1898 The Sun gleefully quotes from a letter received by Aspen broker and owner of the Famous Mine in Lime Gulch, Amos Bourquin, from his brother, former Alderman Gus Bourquin. Gus, who quit Aspen last year for the Klondike, writes: "The country here is not what it was represented. Only a small number will even make expenses." Gus suggests that all still in the United States stay there. The Sun doesn't want Aspen to lose any more residents.

February 5, 1898 Aspen's only national bank, the First National, closes. A new state bank, the Aspen State Bank with only half the First National's capital, takes its place and advertises for former First National customers to move their accounts to it.

February 12, 1898 The Sun claims that a resolution which Senator Teller pushed through the Senate is forcing the McKinleyites to make favorable noises about bi-metallism lest they lose the support of Republican bi-metallists. Even Treasury Secretary Gage, whom the Sun labels the "high priest of goldocracy," is saying that McKinley is a bi-metallist at heart. Noting that a new group of Aspenites is preparing to go to Alaska, the Sun warns that 90% of those who go would not be as lucky as one Cripple Creek man: this man returned with nothing more than a dog to show for a season of hard work and great expenditure! The Sun speculates that the ownership of its arch rival, the Aspen Times, is about to change. It says longtime Times owner, B. Clark Wheeler, is tired of fighting a losing battle. S. I. Hallett, David Hyman's local manager, is rumored to be the new manager of the Times. But the Populist Sun is not rejoicing; such a change means that the right wing of the Democratic Party will be taking over the Times. The Aspen City Council instructs Mayor Nelson and the City Attorney to draw up an ordinance requiring owners of the many vacant buildings in Aspen to secure them against casual entry. Aspen City Physician Dr. Kitchen resigns to go to Alaska, creating a new vacancy for Mayor Nelson to fill. Julia Henry is Treasurer of Aspen's Fortnightly Club, often speaks at the Club's programs.

March 5, 1898 David R. C. Brown visits London to try to sell some of his Aspen mines to the new British company, New Aspen Silver Mines, Ltd. In Aspen, Mayor Nelson calls the Council's attention to the great differences in sewer bills

The Fortnightly Club

ASPEN, COLORADO

PROGRAM

MARCH 26, 1898.

Roll Call—Quotations from Wilhelm Meister.
Readings and Discussion.... .. .. Leader, Mrs. C. A. Wilcox.
Current Topics ....Miss T. W. Browne.

APRIL 9, 1898.

Roll Call—Quotations from famous French Women.
Paper—Women of the French Salon.......... ...Mrs. J. M. Downing.
Current Topics ....Mrs. C. A. Wilcox.

APRIL 29, 1898.

Roll Call—Incidents from the life of Madame De Stael.
Readings and Discussion ....Leader, Mrs. J. M. Downing.
Current Topics....... . ... Mrs. T. B. Kolb.

MAY 7, 1898.

Roll Call Quotations from Bulwer.
Paper—Life of Bulwer............................. Mrs. W. P. Nelson.
Current Topics................................. Mrs. Theo Little, Jr.

MAY 21, 1898.

Roll Call—Character Sketches.
Readings and Discussion .... Leader, Mrs W. P. Nelson.
Current Topics............... .. ..Mrs. J. R Mason.

JUNE 4, 1898.

Roll Call—Quotations from Bacon's Essays.
Paper—Life of Bacon ....Mrs. F O. Smolt.
Current Topics.............................. ....Mrs W. P. Nelson.

JUNE 18, 1898.

Roll Call—Did Bacon write Shakespeare's Plays?
Readings and Discussion...................Leader, Mrs F. O. Smolt.
Current Topics ....Mrs. J. M. Downing.

JULY 2, 1898.

Roll Call Quotations from Ruskin.
Paper—Life of Ruskin..............................Mrs T B Kolb.
Current Topics........ ....Mrs. F. O. Smolt.

JULY 16, 1898.

Roll Call—Gems from Ruskin.
Readings and Discussion.................... Leader, Mrs. T B Kolb.
Current Topics............................ ...... Miss T. W. Browne.

Part of Fortnightly Club Program for 1898

for various properties and recommends harmonization. The City Attorney presents to the Council the requested draft ordinance on securing vacant buildings against entry.

March 12, 1898 The Council rejects the idea of penalizing owners of vacant buildings who do not make them entry-proof, and suggests penalizing trespassers instead. Mayor Nelson calls upon local party heads to submit their lists of judges for the forthcoming municipal elections. The City Marshall breaks into a notorious gambling den over the Brick Saloon on Cooper Street, arresting two and taking the names of others present.

March 19, 1898 Major Champlin, owner of the Hotel Jerome in Aspen and the Vendome Hotel in Leadville, goes bankrupt. The Jerome has been making money, but the Vendome has been a big loser. The City Council appoints three judges in each Aspen precinct for the April 5 election. One judge represents each of the three competing parties, Populists, Democrats and Silver Republicans. Grading is completed for the railway spur to the new Mollie Gibson concentrator. Four carloads of machinery arrive in Aspen on the Colorado Midland, destined for the new marble operation at Conundrum Gulch. Pitkin silver may be in trouble, but marble quarrying is on the upswing in the County, at least for the moment.

April 2, 1898 To save $55 a month, the Aspen City Council proposes to reduce the salaries of the Marshall, the City Clerk, the Police Magistrate and the City Attorney. The Sun reports that Aspen city warrants are trading at 75 to 90 cents on the dollar. Mrs. David R. C. Brown, daughter of pioneer merchant Henry Cowenhoven and wife of Aspen's richest man, dies in Hot Springs, Arkansas. Is all of old Aspen dying?

April 5-9, 1898 In the April 5 municipal elections, Aspen's Fusion Democrats are the big winners. The Populists elect only one of their candidates, longtime City Clerk Alice B. Grover. The Sun blames the People's Party defeat on the decision to chose candidates by primary. Many Aspenites show up at the Wheeler Opera House to see entertainment by the Edison Vitascope Company. Residents along the Roaring Fork River, who have been complaining of pollution, mainly by manure, are told to avoid taking water for domestic purposes below the road bridge. The water will get worse when the new mill of the mine at the head of Hunter Creek begins processing the mine's gold ore. The Aspen City Council assents to a new, uniform schedule of sewer rates proposed by Mayor Nelson. Under it, a two-story private house will pay $10 a year. The Sun welcomes the steady hum of the concentrator now operating at the old Holden Works. Since the concentrator can handle ores with as little as 7 ounces of silver a ton, more Aspen miners may now find work.

April 23, 1898 The first shots are fired in Cuba. The State Department mulls the idea of asking Congress for a formal declaration of war against Spain. In Aspen, the Argentium-Juniata mine closes its surface workings; future mining will be done through the shaft of the Mollie Gibson, the new mill of which will soon start up. Newly elected members of the Aspen City Council take their places. Alderman Stockman is no longer a Council member or Mayor pro tem, but Mayor Nelson still heads the Health Committee. The Aspen Driving and Athletic Association is incorporated, capitalized by 600 shares at $5 apiece. It plans to modernize the old Hallam Land Company track and build a grandstand to bring horse racing to Aspen. New wine in old bottles?

April 30, 1898 In Washington, silver state legislators try, in vain, to amend in a way to benefit silver, bills raising money for the war with Spain. Nonetheless, some speculate that the war may send the price of silver to 75 cents, even 80 cents. In Aspen, new complaints about loose stock are referred to the Ways and Means Committee to decide if a man should again be hired to corral such animals. Aspen learns of the death of another of its leading pioneers, J. C. Hooper. He had arrived in Aspen in 1881, served as People's Party Mayor twice. As Pitkin County Sheriff in 1887-1888, he had taken 18 deputies to Rangely to help the Sheriff there cope with a Ute Indian uprising. His greatest claim to fame came as lessor of the Aspen Mine. He located a rich pocket of ore shortly before his lease ran out, and worked shifts 24 hours a day to get out as much ore as possible while he could.

May 14, 1898 Mrs. B. Clark Wheeler, dies suddenly while at the Excelsior Springs, Missouri spa. Her parents had brought her to Aspen in 1880, where she married Wheeler in 1884. Another old timer is gone. The new Aspen baseball team goes to Glenwood Springs to play its first game. Minus three of the expected players, it recruits substitutes from the crowd. Score: Glenwood Springs 22, Aspen 3. The Aspen City Marshall tells the Council that he has notified drug store owners of the new ordinance calling for them to pay a license fee. He reports that some owners say they will quit rather than pay the $200 a year fee. The company quarrying marble in Conundrum Gulch buys out three conflicting silver claims, and now has clear title to 340 acres there. Silver no longer calls all the shots in Pitkin County.

May 21, 1898 A contractor for the new building of the Denver Mint comes to check out Conundrum Gulch marble. More wheat is sown this year in the Roaring Fork Valley than ever before. At a price of $1.50 a bushel, farmers should clean up. Income from farming and ranching in Pitkin County is replacing income from silver mining.

June 4, 1898 The stamps start up of the new mill at Hunter Pass (at the head of Hunter Creek), putting water quality in the Roaring Fork river at risk. The Sun reports the return of City Attorney Harold Clark and Mayor W. Porter Nelson from Crystal. They traveled "on wheels" from Aspen to that mining camp, and by the same means back to Basalt. Here they caught an Aspen-bound train. From Aspen to Crystal by road down to Carbondale and then up the Crystal River through Marble to Crystal, is over 50 miles; the roads leave much to be desired. It's some bicycle trip! Clark is legal advisor to the Inez Gold and Silver Mining Company with operations at Crystal, and Nelson is an investor in that company.

June 11, 1898 Aspen recruiters are forming two companies of volunteers to go to Cuba. The company recruited by G. E. Rohrbough takes its first drill. The Sun thinks it would be better to recruit only one good company. On Ladies Day at the ball park, Aspen beats Leadville 8 to 2. Fifteen of what the Sun calls "Kodak fiends" meet to organize a camera club and set up a darkroom in Aspen.

June 18, 1898 In Aspen, long time broker E. W. Young

advertises that he wants to buy Argentium-Juniata stock at 26 cents a share.

June 25, 1898 The Aspen City Council cuts the annual dog license fee from $3.00 to $1.50.

July 2, 1898 The American assault on Santiago de Cuba begins. In Aspen, broker E. W. Young advertises to buy Aspen municipal warrants, no price stated. Warrants are promises to pay that the city uses to pay bills when it lacks immediate cash, which happens often.

July 9, 1898 American casualties in Cuba reach 2,000. Broker E. W. Young turns his Aspen office over to employee Andy Mulqueen while he personally opens a new office in Colorado Springs. That city has an active exchange for mining stocks, trading Aspen shares as well as Cripple Creek speculations. Some 3,000 persons turn out for the July 4 races at Aspen's new horse racing track. Admission, 50 cents for adults, 25 cents for children.

July 16, 1898 Mayor Nelson releases from jail the sole drunk arrested over the July 4 holiday. Nelson attends the weekly meeting of the Pitkin County Board vice City Treasurer McNichols, when an Aspen tax matter is discussed. Four Aspenites return to Aspen from Crystal via Maroon Pass, bemoaning the lack of a good road between the two.

July 23, 1898 Mayor Nelson appoints a committee of three to study the complaints received about the new sewer rates. Looking at Crystal mining possibilities are the son-in-law of big Aspen investor, Jerome B. Wheeler, along with Aspen grocer Frank Meyer, and the Assistant Superintendent of the Mollie Gibson and Argentium-Juniata mines.

August 6, 1898 Ignoring the pollution, the Sun terms the Hunter Pass gold operations the "sheet anchor" of Pitkin County. Former Alderman Bourquin, now in St. Michaels, Alaska, on his way home from Dawson in the Yukon, says he won't go back to the Klondike, at least not anytime soon.

August 8, 1898 In Duluth, Charles A. Townes, head of the Silver Republican National Committee, states that the soon-to-be issued report of the Indian Silver Commission will recommend reopening the Indian mints to the coinage of silver, but at a 22:1 silver-to-gold ratio calculated to leave existing Indian price levels undisturbed.

August 12, 1898 In Washington, an agreement is signed ending the war between the United States and Spain. The French Ambassador signs for Spain, and the Secretary of State for the United States.

August 13, 1898 The English company, New Aspen Silver Mines, Ltd., records deeds to three more silver mining claims. The former Aspen City Physician, Dr. Kitchen, returns to Aspen from Alaska where he had gone to practice. He found on his arrival that there were 15 doctors in Skagway. He says he can find more work to do in two days in Aspen than during a whole month in Skagway. The Sun reports that W. Porter Nelson's niece, Kate Nelson, is returning to her home in Kansas City after visiting her uncle. She is the 20-year-old daughter of Nelson's older half-brother, Lucian M. Nelson.

August 20, 1898 Citing with approval the Washington Post's prediction that the Democrats, the Populists and the Silver Republicans will fight the 1900 elections on the same slogans as in 1896, the Sun calls the Post one of the few of the few unbiased papers in the East. A prominent jeweler pulls up stakes in Aspen, and moves his business to Riverside, California. The new concentrator at the Smuggler Mine is being expanded. The Aspen City Council considers a petition to allow a citizen to work off his $1 poll tax by sending a substitute. Merchants often want to meet poll tax obligations by sending one of the many men owing them money to do street work in their place. In Crystal, the Inez mine has 12 men working and is opening good ore bodies.

August 27, 1898 Smuggler mine manager Samuel I. Hallett gets a United States patent on his "Hallett table", an important part of the Smuggler's ore concentrator. The silver price averages 59.54 cents in August, 1898 vs. 54.19 cents an ounce in August, 1897, and 67.34 cents an ounce in August, 1896. Not a boom, but at least off the bottom. When Aspen asks for bids on supplies of lime to carry out the city's annual privy disinfection, two druggists submit identical bids. Mayor Nelson resolves the ensuing problem by asking the two suppliers to decide themselves how to divide the business.

September 3, 1898 Peoples Party activists meet at the Aspen City Hall to select delegates to a special state convention in Colorado Springs where fusion of all silverite parties will be discussed. Mayor Nelson becomes leader of the delegation.

September 10, 1898 Mayor Nelson tells the Sun that there is no truth to the story floating around that he sold a property in the Cripple Creek District for $50,000. He says that the property has only been leased, and $30,000 was the amount of bond posted. The property has no surface ore showings, but is valued for being near some good workings.

September 17, 1898 At special conventions in Colorado Springs, the three pro-silver parties agree on joint action. The Sun writes that the Colorado Democrats are now relieved of the incubus of Clevelandism, while regular Republicans will have to fight clearly under the gold flag. Other states should follow Colorado's example. Aspen schools grow: 150 more students this year than last. The Aspen City Council proposes a new ordinance requiring street peddlers to be licensed. About 100 men are working in the Aspen mine on day wages; others are working for themselves in leased portions of the mine. In Crystal, the Schofield smelter is being expanded. One Aspen resident owning a mine in Crystal says that the Hoffman Smelting Company paid him $140 for just four days' output. Papers are filed in Pitkin County for the incorporation of a Crystal River Railroad Company, capitalized at $1,000,000, with shares to cost $100 each. The railroad has ambitious plans, not only to put rails into the promising mining town of Crystal and beyond, but also to construct a number of branch lines into various side valleys.

September 24, 1898 The Sun prints a joint letter from the chairmen of the Colorado Democratic, Peoples and Silver Republican parties bidding other states to copy the example of the Colorado fusion agreement of September 8, 1898. Aspen merchants petition the City council to pass the ordinance requiring street hawkers to buy a $150 license. Essentially the same group of people call for rescinding the Council rule that the poll tax be paid either in cash, or one day's personal service, without allowing any substitutes.

October 1, 1898 Some Aspen men take over the Eureka mine in the Crystal district, situated at an altitude in excess of 14,000 feet. The Sun reports that Mayor Nelson is visiting Crystal to look at his mining interests there. The Aspen Consolidated Mining Company, incorporated in Kansas, receives from the Land Office placer mining patents on 180 acres adjoining the town. In the City Council, Mayor Nelson opposes the proposed license for peddlers on the grounds the peddlers perform a service for people who cannot get out to shop, and on the grounds of conflict with Colorado law. He casts the deciding negative vote when the Council divides three to three on the ordinance.

October 22, 1898 J. B. Wheeler reaches a settlement with the creditors of his failed Aspen bank, thus removing this bankruptcy case from court purview. Wheeler will later recall that he paid his depositors 100 cents on the dollar. Porter Nelson records his sale of interests in the Last Chance and Lucky Queen lodes in the Roaring Fork mining district.

October 29, 1898 Andy Barnett, one of the owners of the Lead King mine in Crystal, ships 1,600 pounds of sample ore to London to see if Britishers might invest. He pays $36 to get the ore shipment to the railhead at Carbondale, but only $23 from there to London. Oh, how Crystal could use a direct railroad connection with the outside world!

November 8, 1898 Republicans win the off year elections, maintaining control of Congress. W. J. Bryan comments that "silver is stronger than ever . . . Perhaps our opponents will now admit that silver is not dead. The attempt to secure international bi-metallism has proved a failure, and it is now more apparent then ever before that Americans must legislate for themselves on this question." In Colorado, the fusion parties win. Republican B. Clark Wheeler loses his bid to become a member of the House of Representatives, and Republican Edward Wolcott loses his bid to be Governor.

November 12, 1898 Roaring Fork valley ranchers report a number of cattle deaths. Six Denver Rio Grande railroad workers die of poisoning contracted at their rooming house, which draws its water from the Roaring Fork River. The new concentrator at Aspen is blamed for polluting the river.

November 19, 1898 Edgar Bassick, son the owner of the legendary Bassick silver mine near Rosita, Colorado, visits his Aspen cousin, Charles Ellis. They inspect the new mill and concentrator at the Smuggler mine, which S. I. Hallett has designed to extract more lead from silver ore. The silver price is so low that extracting and selling the lead contained in many Aspen silver ores is increasingly important.

November 26, 1898 In Washington, the Bureau of Printing and Engraving begins issuing silver certificates of a new design. The Aspen City Council, always looking for money, considers a proposal to raise the license fee on the Wheeler Opera House from $100 to $200 a year.

December 17, 1898 Eaton Goodall quits Aspen to work at the Bassick Mine near Rosita. Shareholders of Aspen's Little Annie mine want to throw it into receivership. The Bonnybelle mine is sold at a sheriff's sale for $5,500. Smuggler manager Samuel I. Hallett meets in Basalt with ranchers irate over the pollution of the Roaring Fork River, and tells them that Aspen will do all it can to minimize the problem. The Aspen City Council considers imposing a special $5 tax on arrangers of any theatrical performance where the admission is 50 cents or more. Mayor Nelson opposes the tax, arguing that performers really take very little money out of the city, and that performances create jobs for many city residents. He casts the deciding negative vote when the Council divides three to three.

<u>December 23, 1898</u> A Chicago paper says that the head of the Illinois Democratic Party is planning to abandon his past support of silver to join forces with the New York gold bugs.

<u>December 24, 1898</u> B. X. Dawson, who played first base for the Aspen team last summer, discovers a rich gold area near Canon City. New Aspen Silver Mines, Ltd. begins working some of its Beaver State properties. The Crystal River Railroad mortgages all its property for one year, at an interest rate of 8%, to get money for further construction.

<u>Year end, 1898</u> Aspen is enjoying such winter sports as tobogganing and ice skating at Hallam Lake, despite fears that small pox may spread to the city from an epidemic in Eastern Colorado. No skiing yet.

<u>January 2, 1899</u> Although the Monday after New Years is a legal holiday in Colorado, Mayor Nelson convenes the City Council. The Council instructs Mayor Nelson's Health Committee to cooperate with Pitkin County in locating an inexpensive house for possible use as a "pest house" for small

pox. Mineral production in Pitkin County, lead excepted, decreases in 1898 as compared with 1897. Read the following figures while remembering that in 1892 before Sherman Act repeal, Pitkin silver output exceeded $5,800,000:

	1897	1898
Silver	$2,744,000.	$2,319,000.
Gold	169,000.	71,000.
Lead	151,000.	577,000.
Copper	800.	596.

January 16, 1899 The Aspen City Council meets to receive a report about the poll tax collector's activities since December 1. He has taken in $66 in cash, and persuaded 10 persons to pay the tax through work. Since the collector keeps 25% of all that he collects, he retains $19 and turns $47 into the city treasury. The City Council decides to attend in mass the funeral of former Council member Gus Bourquin, who died shortly after returning to Aspen from a year in the Klondike.

January 21, 1899 The Sun denies the rumors that small pox has struck Aspen. The Crystal River Railroad plans to stock the Crystal River with 100,000 trout fry in the hope of promoting tourist traffic. The railroad welcomes mining activity, but says it will insist that mills and reduction works not pollute. Aspen is ambivalent about pollution from mining.

January 28, 1899 Shame on Aspen! Glenwood Springs residents say that the Roaring Fork River is once again black, after six weeks of being clear. Aspen takes from Leadville the record for the largest load of ore hauled when a sleigh drawn by four horses moves 31,100 pounds net of ore from the

Aspen Mining and Smelting Company property on Aspen Mountain to the Taylor and Bruton Sampling Works. The Sun says that the many Aspenites who took their chances that the County might sell their property in the November 2, 1898 tax sale will be surprised when they learn that, for the first time since 1893, outside capital has bought Aspen property. Since 1893, the County has had little success in attracting new buyers when it advertised delinquent properties for sale. The County then usually negotiates with the original owners to get them to pay a much reduced tax bill. Porter Nelson loses two of his Aspen properties to a mysterious out-of-town buyer. The Aspen City Council again receives many complaints about horses and cattle loose in the City, and authorizes Mayor Nelson to hire a new stock policeman. The Council also receives many complaints about coal and water sleighs breaking up walks going about their business. The Council instructs the City Marshall to stop this.

February 4, 1899 Word reaches Aspen that most Colorado smelters are uniting in a combine. Some Aspen mine owners brag that they can get by for months without shipping any ore to smelters. Many problems with heavy snows: eighteen horses are killed by a snow slide on the road to Independence; two aldermen can't make it to the regular Monday meeting of the City Council because of snow. The Council backtracks somewhat on its instructions to Marshall Likens to enforce a ban on sleighs crossing walks. The Council agrees to allow the driver of the steam thawing apparatus to cross walks to carry out his business, provided he does this before 8 A.M.. The driver had been fined $3 under the previous rule.

February, 1899 Heavy snow continues to fall, blocking all rail lines into Aspen. Telephone and telegraph lines go down as well. Some say this is the heaviest snowfall since at least 1884. Aspen alleys are so full of snow shoveled off roofs that the fire department can't reach many places. With all transport cut, city coal supplies become critical. Smuggler manager Hallett says his operations have plenty of coal, but can't share it. The high price of lead requires that his mines go on working and using that coal. Volunteers are called out on a Sunday to shovel the rails towards Glenwood Springs, especially the route of the Colorado Midland. The Midland offers the most direct way of getting coal into Aspen. The Denver and Rio Grande Railroad agrees to transport shovelers to stops at Ten Mile and Snow Mass, where the snow problems are the greatest. One hundred volunteers turn out to work on the Rio Grande, and 250 on the Midland. The Sun says that Mayor Nelson, John Nash and Ed Ogden (owner of the Aspen Drygoods Company) are such vigorous shovelers that ordinary folk should stay away from them to avoid any avalanche danger! By 6 P.M., the volunteers open the lines critical to coal. A train with four cars of coal and three cars of shovelers starts back to Aspen from Basalt. The load proves to be too great, and two cars of coal have to be dropped. The train finally makes it back to Aspen at 8:30 P.M.. City coal supplies gradually are built up. Smuggler Manager Hallett now wants to accumulate a supply of 1,000 tons of coal before spring floods can cause a new shortage.

February 11, 1899 The Crystal River Railroad plans to start bridge abutment work along its right of way before spring floods make this impossible. The stage line up the Crystal River is still unable to go above Marble; mail is taken to

Crystal on snowshoe. Leadville recaptures the ore hauling record for one team; it is now 37,150 pounds. The Aspen City Council decides to protest a bill being considered by the Colorado Legislature in Denver requiring that cities of second class such as Aspen obtain bids for electricity. Aspen has a municipal electric plant, the Peoples Power and Light Company, to provide competition for the Roaring Fork Electric Company owned by David R. C. Brown. The Council fears if it must take bids, Brown will underbid the municipal plant just to drive it out of business and then raise his rates.

<u>February 18, 1899</u> One Charles K. Phillips of Denver is revealed to be the mysterious buyer of so many Aspen properties in the November 2, 1888 Pitkin County tax sale.

<u>February 25, 1899</u> Hoping for new tax revenues, Mayor Nelson and Pitkin County Assessor Anderson complete a study showing that railway property in Colorado is underassessed for tax purposes. Mayor Nelson receives a letter from the President of the Denver Conservatory and College of Music asking about city interest in hosting a summer session of the College of Music. Note: a summer music festival is proposed a half century before the Aspen Music Festival comes into being! The City Council decides that the 1899 poll tax can be considered paid if property owners clean out the ditches along their property, after having made prior arrangement with Aspen's Street Supervisor. Aspen residents no longer have to go to Glenwood Springs for a hot bath; a Turkish bath opens in Aspen's Lincoln block. Mollie Gibson is one of only two actively traded Aspen stocks on the Colorado Springs stock exchange; Gibson shares cost 27 cents, far less than earlier. At its annual meeting in Council Bluffs, Iowa, the Gibson

management tells shareholders it made a profit of over $31,000 in 1898, despite the low price of silver.

March 4, 1899 The annual report of the Argentium-Juniata company shows that in 1898, it paid off its debt and built up a cash surplus of over $32,700. The stock is priced at 33 cents a share. Mayor Nelson informs the City Council of a bill pending in the state legislature which would limit the amount of tax various counties could levy. In the case of Pitkin County, the levy will be capped at 15 mills vs. the 17.5 mills currently set. The Council takes no action.

March 18, 1899 Interest builds up in advance of Aspen's coming municipal election. Three parties, Peoples, Democrats and Silver Republicans, nominate candidates for municipal offices; Mayor Nelson does not run again. The Silver Republicans show affinity for the Democrats by accepting the Democratic candidate for City Treasurer as their candidate. For the first time in his almost two years as Mayor, Nelson misses a City Council meeting; he is in Denver with a sick Edgar Stallard, his colleague from Culpeper, Virginia.

March 25, 1899 Mayor Nelson is back presiding over the regular Monday Aspen City Council meeting. The Council approves the ordinance charging second hand dealers a license fee of $60 a year, and instructs the City Attorney to initiate steps to get a Federal patent for East Aspen. Meanwhile, the Democratic nominee for mayor withdraws. Job not attractive?

April 1, 1899 A new law passed by the Colorado state legislature reduces from 8% to 6% the interest cities like Aspen can pay on their warrants. Farmers in the Roaring

Fork valley are again threatening to take Aspen to court for polluting the river. The Sun says that Aspenites should greet farmers "with an icy stare" when they come into town to sell their produce. The Council approves the 1899 budget for Aspen: $26,000, down $2,000 from 1898. Voters registered for the coming Aspen election number 1,678.

April 8, 1899 John McNeill of the Peoples Party is elected Mayor of Aspen, succeeding Nelson. The new City Council is expected to be more relaxed about gambling in the city.

April 15, 1899 In London, a Blue Book appears with the findings of the Indian Currency Commission Inquiry. The book reveals that six months earlier, Secretary of State John Hay had not rejected an idea put forward by a leading British bi-metallist that the Indian Mint should coin silver at the ratio of 22 ounces of silver equal one ounce of gold. In Aspen, the City Council instructs Marshall Likens to begin, as of Wednesday, to impound loose horses and cattle, and to find a suitable location for holding the stock. Many properties of the Aspen Mining and Smelting Company, controlled by Jerome B. Wheeler, are sold in lots at a sheriff's sale. One lot, including the Spar, Emma and 25 other properties, brings $20,000. Three other lots bring $1,000 each. One lot gets no bids. Wheeler and other shareholders protest the sale, in vain.

April 22, 1899 The Denver Post editorializes about the rumors that the Ute Indians will again make a summer hunting excursion from their Utah reservation into their old Western Colorado hunting grounds. The Post says that if those charged with keeping the Utes on their reservation can't do it, the Utes should be moved further away from Colorado.

Porter Nelson,
Aspen,
c. 1890

Julia Henry
Nelson, Aspen,
c. 1890

"Henry" (Julia) Nelson, Aspen, c. 1898

Julia Henry Nelson, Denver, 1918

Porter Nelson, as member of the Aspen School Board, 1906-10

Porter Nelson, Mulford, Co., October, 1940

Porter, Julia Henry on a kids's picnic, c. 1895

The Nelson kids, c. 1898. From the left: Kate, Carmer, Marguerite

Nelson home, w. Hallam, Aspen, c.1900

Nelson Parlor, Aspen

The Aspen Nelsons visit the Culpeper Nelsons, 1900
At the top left, Julia Henry. Clockwise from bottom right: Kate, Marguerite, Porter, Carmer

The dog is Bob, Aspen, c. 1901

Nelsons at home, Aspen, c. 1901

Watermelon picnic, Aspen, 1905
Porter (left), Julia Henry (right)

Nelsons at Aspen station, July, 1906, From right: Porter, Kate, Marguerite, Julia Henry

Aspen prospectors in Nevada,
Nye County, 1907

Porter Nelson, prospecting, Nevada, 1907

Colorado Highland Marble Quarry,
November, 1914

Nelson's downtown Aspen building,
The "Aspen Block," 1996 view

Porter Nelson (left) with Echternach, Houston grandchildren, Cottonwood Lakes, CO., 1936

Last known photo of Porter Nelson Hotchkiss, CO, December, 1943 Nelson at the right.

Hotel at Crystal, 1902

Jack train animals, Main Street,
Crystal, 1902

Julia Henry (center), Porter (right)
Crystal, c. 1905

Mrs. Cottrell, her two children, in front of her miners boarding house, Crystal, July, 1923

Porter Nelson (with cap), Crystal, c. 1905

Crystal from Black Queen Trail, 1932

Main street and hotel, Crystal, c. 1930
Porter Nelson's Lucky Boy mine, top left

Nelson cabin, Crystal

Sheep Mountain power plant, left, and mill, right. Part of what Nelson wants to sell in 1940

Entrance to Nelson's Inez mine, Crystal

Mayor Nelson opens an Aspen City Council meeting for the last time, thanking all Council members for their cooperation during his term. He surrenders the office to his successor, and turns over the remaining city funds placed earlier in his personal checking account. The first Midland train in eleven weeks to make it through the snows on the Continental Divide reaches Aspen. The Little Annie properties will be sold by the sheriff to satisfy creditors.

April 29, 1899 A wagon train leaves Aspen to try to reach the few men who wintered over at the Hunter Pass mine. They are out of all provisions except for flour and potatoes. If the melt continues, the mine could resume operations in three weeks.

May 6, 1899 On Main Street in Aspen, workers hired by the city begin tearing up rails of the defunct street railway, abandoned some time ago by its promoters.

May 20, 1899 The engineer for the Crystal River Railroad confirms that snow run off has damaged the roadbed, but says it is not serious. The furniture of Aspen's Clarendon Hotel is sold by the sheriff to satisfy a county tax claim.

May 27, 1899 W. Porter Nelson, F. H. Stockman and Jacob Sands find wide acceptance for their idea of forming a home mining company to look for and develop valuable mineral deposits, especially of gold, thought to exist near Aspen. Leadville already has such a home mining company. Nelson urges that the company be started promptly to take advantage of the five months of prospecting weather remaining. Others think that the new company should not engage in prospecting but instead just consider offers of already discovered mineral deposits. Aspen businessman will be asked to subscribe $5 to $25 a month to start the enterprise. The baseball game at Aspen between the local team and Leadville is called in the third inning. Why? Snow! In Aspen, it's not unusual in May.

June 1, 1899 Defeated Democratic Presidential candidate William Jennings Bryan tells the Ohio Bi-metallic League that he still favors free coinage of silver.

June 3, 1899 At the organizational meeting of the Home Mining Company, Porter Nelson nominates R. G. Withers to be Chairman; the nomination is approved unanimously.

June 10, 1899 The Board of Directors of the Home Mining Company, now formally named the Aspen Mine Prospecting and Development Company, meets at the office of W. Porter Nelson in the Aspen block. T. J. Flynn is named President, J. Sands Vice President and W. Porter Nelson, who knows a lot about organizational matters, is made Secretary.

June 17, 1899 H. W. Clark, and Mr. and Mrs. W. Porter Nelson return to Aspen from Crystal where they attended a shareholders meeting of the Inez Mining Company. The Sun comments that the troubled expression on Nelson's face is not the result of the smelter closing, but rather the prospect of a damage suit against him. A few days ago when he was en route to Glenwood Springs by bicycle, he ran into the side of bridge about a mile below Carbondale, damaging the structure. A short time thereafter, the bridge collapsed when fifteen head of cattle were crossing, throwing all into the river. Three were drowned. Nelson says that if he can pay for the cattle as cheaply as the railroads do, he won't fight a suit should one be brought against him. Subsequently, the Sun reports that someone made off with Nelson's "ice wagon" cycle. The paper opines that a friend may have taken it to give the owner a rest. Aspen Mine Prospecting and Development Company directors again meet in the office of W. Porter Nelson. They decide that where not paid for outright, company shares can be bought for 1/5th down and the rest at 1/5 a month for four months. As Secretary, Nelson is told to procure record books and stationery for the new company, and to receive written offers from persons wanting to sell claims. Due to the Denver smelter strike, the Taylor and Bruton Sampling Company suspends purchase of ores in Aspen. Samuel I. Hallett says his mines will continue to work nevertheless. William Derry of New Aspen Silver Mines, Ltd. comes from London to view that company's Aspen operations.

June 24, 1899 The directors of the Aspen Mine Prospecting and Development Company appoint a committee consisting of R. G. Withers, E. L. Ogden and W. Porter Nelson to draft a letter setting forth the purposes of the Company and soliciting investors. The park at Hallam Lakes has been cleared up after the heavy winter snows, and will reopen with a Grand Ball, music to be provided by Daggett's Orchestra. Admission is free. Aspen is alive, again.

July 1, 1899 National representatives of the three political parties which supported the Bryan platform of 1896 visit Aspen to raise funds for a free silver, anti-monopoly campaign in 1900. For $500 and the assumption of debt, the Aspen Consolidated Mining Company takes over the Famous Mine and concentrator from B. Clark Wheeler. The Sun reports that the Nelson family is going to Glenwood Springs by train, while Nelson himself is going there by bicycle with J. F. MacMillan. The water level in the Roaring Fork, down three to four feet from its week ago high, still is dangerous.

July 15, 1899 The Aspen City Council debates whether the city should work with the Argentium-Juniata mine to seek from the General Land Office a town site patent for East Aspen, or go it alone in fighting the so-called Ensign claim to part of East Aspen. The A-J company holds a mining claim in East Aspen which conflicts with the Ensign claim. The Aspen Consolidated Mining Company gets three leases from B. Clark Wheeler for Little Annie property. The deeds reveal, for the first time, that Wheeler is the President and Manager of the Aspen Consolidated Mining Company which has been taking up new mining patents around Aspen.

July 22, 1899 The concentrator at the old Holden Works is started up by the new owners, who are from Denver and Colorado Springs. The Sun reports that M. C. McNichols, T. A. Curry and W. Porter Nelson are going Crystal to look after their mining interests there.

July 29, 1899 Mayor McNeill and his predecessor as Mayor, W. Porter Nelson, go up Castle Creek on behalf of the new Home Mining Company to investigate a property in the Montezuma district. They bring back some promising ore samples for testing. Directors of that Company hear a lecture from an expert on mineral formation. More than 1,000 persons turn out to view a bicycle race arranged by the Glenwood Springs Wheel Club to Basalt. The Aspen

Lawn Tennis Club, to which ex-Mayor Nelson belongs, is operating a court at the corner of Center and Francis Streets.

August 8, 1899 Former Missouri Governor Stone tells the Democratic National Committee in Chicago that the Party should cut its ties to the People's Party and the Silver Republicans. In London, the Secretary of State for India announces the Government's conclusion that India should go on the gold standard. He explains that the talks in 1897 with France and the US about a bi-metallic standard had been fruitless, and that 80% of India's trade is with gold standard countries. Aspen mines, still suffering from the cessation of ore purchases caused by the Denver smelter strike, ship small qualities of high grade ore to smelters in Utah and Omaha.

August 19, 1899 Glenwood Springs turns out to welcome home Colorado soldiers returning from Manila. Aspen Mayor McNeill, W. Porter Nelson and Charles Bott leave for the Independence, Difficult Creek and Lincoln Gulch mining areas to look at mining properties offered to the Home Mining Company. The Aspen Consolidated Mining Company obtains a patent on the Lux placer. The Aspen City Council learns that the General Land Office has denied the Mollie Gibson company a patent on the Browder Lode, because the Browder claim conflicts with the East Aspen town site patent.

August 26, 1899 The Chicago Tribune says that Chicago banks are suffering from the annual outflow of small currency to the farming areas. Farmers employ lots of extra labor at the harvest season and regularly drain small value money from the city at this time of year. The Denver smelter strike is over. Smelters have begun purchasing ore, but only 60 of the

400 car loads of ore accumulated during the strike have so far been moved out of Aspen. The Hunter Pass Mining Company will shut down as soon as low water stops it from generating electricity for the mill there. Messrs. McNeill, Nelson and Bott return to Aspen with ore samples from the properties they investigated for the Home Mining Company. From the pages of the Sun: "W. Porter Nelson has lost his mascot and he will not happy or lucky until he finds it. It was a silver dollar with a history and a monogram. The monogram is borne in plain view on the eagle's breast-the letters `JCN.' The history Mr. Nelson tells only to his intimate friends. This remarkable dollar told the time of day better than a watch, if the sun was shining; by its prophetic "flip" its owner could tell with accuracy when to buy or sell stocks, or start with safety on a journey. Its virtues were limited only by the demands placed on it, but it is gone now and its whilom owner is disconsolate. He unthinkingly paid it out Tuesday instead of a commonplace, everyday dollar with which his pockets are always well provided and did not miss it until he was called upon to make a momentous decision. Mr. Nelson will reward the party who will restore to him his mascot." Carelessness is human.

September 2, 1899 The organizers of the Paris World Exhibition ask Aspen to send a good exhibit of local minerals. The City Council learns that David R. C. Brown is ready to negotiate the sale of his ditch and water rights in East Aspen.

September 9, 1899 The Sun reports that Treasury Secretary Gage received two designs for a new $5 silver certificate, one with a likeness of Washington and the other with Jefferson.

Then a Republican Senator prevails on Gage to reject the Jefferson design. Jefferson was a Democrat!

September 16, 1899 David R. C. Brown sells his East Aspen water supply to the city for $150. An early snow storm knocks down standing grain along Brush Creek.

September 23, 1899 The Sun reports the return of H. W. Clark and W. Porter Nelson from a ten-day bicycle trip of more than 700 miles, from Aspen to Carbondale to Crystal, then over the range to Gunnison, down the Black Canyon of the Gunnison to Montrose, on to Ouray, Silverton, Telluride, Rico and Creede, thence to Salida and Buena Vista. Their return to Aspen was over 11,000 foot high Independence Pass. The Sun reports that Mrs. W. Porter Nelson gave a dance at her home. Now the bad news: Peru, a great silver mining country, adopts the gold standard. The Sun's comment: Peru like India owes the Rothschilds so much money that they have to do what they are told. The paper says that silver mining is as good an industry as any other; the US government should just create a market for its product.

September 30, 1899 Millionaire David R. C. Brown offers his grand residence on Hallam Street to the County for a school, orphanage or whatever. The price: $5,000 in school warrants yielding 5 ½%. If Brown leaves Aspen, should Porter Nelson stay?

October 7, 1899 Attorney R. G. Withers, earlier elected Chairman of the Home Mining Company, is opening a law office in Cripple Creek. The Acting City Physician reports three cases of typhoid fever in West Aspen along the Castle Creek ditch. The Council accepts his recommendation to shut down the ditch to prevent the spread of the dread disease.

October 14, 1899 The Sun says there is no basis for the belief that the outbreak of war between England and the Boers of South Africa will cause a depression in Cripple Creek. The Directors of the Home Mining Company appoint a committee of four - Henry Beck, E. L. Ogden, George Marchland and W. Porter Nelson - to meet with local merchants to solicit share subscriptions to support an active mining campaign. To date, the Directors have met company expenses from their own pockets. They can tell would-be investors that the Leadville Home Mining company has been a success, with its shares now fetching $3.50. Taking note that persons outside Aspen turned the water back on in the Castle Creek ditch, the Aspen City Council votes to close it again.

October 21, 1899 Populists of Pitkin County hold their convention. Fred H. Stockman is named Chairman of the convention's Resolutions Committee. The convention adopts a resolution of sympathy for the Boers in South Africa, who are described as fighting against an oppressive power. The convention votes down a motion favoring fusion with other pro-silver parties. Porter Nelson becomes a member of the Executive Committee of the Pitkin County Peoples Party.

October 28, 1899 The Sun editorializes about Admiral Dewey of Manila Bay fame: "Dewey is still the hero of the hour and still his name is sounded by his ambitious personal friends as a presidential candidate. But he says that he does not want political honor, and everyone knows that Hanna is glad he does not . . . Dewey would be likely to give the Republican Party managers a severe attack of nervous prostration if he were their candidate." Shades of General Colin Powell in 1996? The Sun reports that plans are being drawn up for the construction of a new Western Slope smelter. It will be located in Grand Junction, and will be Colorado's largest.

November 4, 1899 Both of Aspen's remaining milliners leave town for good. The Sun attacks the McKinley speech at Ackley, Iowa, in which the President said that the United States was permanently on a gold basis. The Sun: Republicans fooled people in 1896 by running a platform friendly to international bi-metallism. Now that McKinley and his advisers think they are firmly entrenched, they boldly hoist the yellow flag. No reason for Silver Republicans to stick with their party, concludes the paper.

November 11, 1899 The Populists win the Pitkin County elections. Aspen's Shakespeare Club meets at the home of Mrs. Davis H. Waite, wife of the former People's Party Governor of Colorado. D. R. C. Brown is looking for a home in Denver. His daughters, each to inherit $3 million from their mother, are attending finishing school in Paris.

November 18, 1899 The Sun charges that every Republican newspaper in the United States "strongly supports the British in their outrageous war upon the industrious and thrifty Dutch of the Transvaal Republic." Over 60 men come into the Roaring Fork valley to build a telephone line between Aspen and Glenwood Springs. Aspenites observe for several seconds a large "aerolite" descending over Red Mountain about 7 P.M.. It is very brilliant and leaves a greenish trail behind as it sinks. This before the Air Force or anyone else started sending up weather balloons, "flying saucers," etc.

November 25, 1899 Financial circles in New York complain of a shortage of money. This is not caused by rural areas demanding money to move their crops, nor does the money seem to have gone to any other region. The Sun thinks that perhaps the money went to finance investments in Cuba or Puerto Rico, and calls upon Congress to do something to add to the money supply. It urges that silver have a role here. Ute Indians stage a raid into the White River area of Colorado they used to occupy, protesting the recent killing of two braves and squaw by game wardens. Since the Utes had paid financial compensation for killing Indian agent Meeker, they argue that now they should receive money compensation. Broker E. W. Young, who some time ago moved the bulk of his operations to Colorado Springs, sells the remaining interest in his Aspen office to longtime employee Andy Mulqueen. With the proceeds, Young will open a new brokerage office in Salt Lake City. The Sun urges Aspenites to give their stock orders to Andy Mulqueen. Big Aspen investor, Jerome B. Wheeler, negotiates with creditors to win back control of the properties sold by the Sheriff to satisfy the claims of the William Wood heirs. Wood now is in an insane asylum in Kansas. Wheeler agrees to give the Wood beneficiaries $56,000 secured by liens on certain property and a 1/16 interest in the Emma Mine which Wood's father had located. Wheeler also promises them a share in the profits of the Aspen Mining and Smelting Company which Wheeler will keep operating. The Sun says that the 81 acres on Aspen Mountain held by Aspen Mining and Smelting Company are worth more money than at any time in the past. It predicts that Wheeler will again be rich and that his faith in Aspen, through thick and thin, will be amply rewarded. The Aspen City Council fails to hold its regular Monday meeting. Mayor McNeill is in Victor working on an about-to-expire lease of a gold mine. R. G. Withers, elected Chairman of the Aspen Home Mining Company when the company was formed, is now active in Cripple Creek. Former Aspenite and former Governor Davis H. Waite is also in Cripple Creek. The Home Mining Company has disappeared from the news. Last Aspen resident to leave: please turn off the lights!

<u>December 9, 1899</u> Pitkin County voters reject, by an 111 to 72 referendum vote, the offer of David R. C. Brown to sell his mansion to the County for a school. Brown huffily calls for bids to tear his Hallam Street house down to save on taxes. In the end, the house will remain and become Aspen High school. Frank Bulkely, long time Aspen agent for Jerome B. Wheeler, resigns his post. While some things change in Aspen, some things continue. Example: the suit of Roaring Fork ranchers against Aspen mill managers for polluting the Roaring Fork river is continued, until February.

<u>December 23, 1899</u> A suit demanding the coinage of silver bullion is filed with the Colorado Supreme Court. The <u>Sun</u> attacks McKinley's message to Congress for its endorsement of the mono-metallic gold standard. The papers charges that as soon as the gold standard bill passes, the country can expect a general cut in wages. Long time Aspen City Clerk Alice B. Grover, a Populist, resigns.

<u>March 14, 1900</u> The US formally endorses the gold standard in the Gold Standard Act (31 Stat. 45). The Act bars the

issuance of silver certificates in denominations larger than $10. It provides for the minting of excess silver bullion which the Treasury bought under the Sherman Act. Sops to Silverites: the legal tender nature of the silver dollar, as then provided by law, is not to be impaired, and international bi-metallism is not barred, if the major commercial nations agree on it.

April 2, 1900 Julia Henry, in Baltimore with her three children for some weeks visiting her mother, Mrs. James W. Carmer, writes to Porter Nelson in Aspen. Her disappointment shows through at Porter's delay in coming East: "If you expect to leave Aspen about the middle of April, that will bring you here too late for Easter, but I suppose it can't be helped. . . I expect we will all enjoy going back by way of Galveston." She is concerned about the children missing more school due to Porter's delayed arrival, but says if they get back to Aspen by May, "I guess they can make it."

April 22, 1900 Julia Henry's purchase is recorded in Gunnison County of a 1/8th interest in the Twilight lode, the Quartz Creek Mining district. From this date until after her death, all Nelson purchases of mining property in Gunnison County are made in her name, not Porter's. Why is that?

June, 1900 The 12th Decennial Census reveals much about Aspen sociology. Most of the Aspenites whose names appear in the Aspen press live in West Aspen. Like the Porter Nelsons (not in the 1900 Aspen census), these newsworthy families typically are in their late 30's or early 40's, with families begun after coming to Aspen. The census shows that native-born American residents come from as far away as Maine, as close as Missouri. Few are from the deep south.

A number of store or saloon owners are immigrants. David R. C. Brown, an immigrant from Canada, is recorded as living on Galena Street, and described as a "capitalist." But West Aspen is not home exclusively to the well off. Lawyer and former Governor of Colorado, Davis H. Waite (at 75, very old for Aspen) is recorded as living at 212 West Illinois, but a construction laborer is shown as living in the house at 219 West Illinois. Mining engineer Samuel I. Hallett, David Hyman's local representative, lives at 430 West Francis with his wife, two nieces and a nephew; a miner lies at 412 West Francis. Real estate agent Edgar Stallard lives at 528 West Main; a miner lives at 526 West Main. Down from 8,800 in 1890, Pitkin's population is counted as 7,020 in the 1900 census, half of whom live in Aspen city.

Political conventions, 1900: Meeting in Philadelphia, the Republicans renominate McKinley. The Republican platform restates allegiance to the gold standard and declares steadfast opposition to the Democrat's idea of free and unlimited coinage of silver. The Republicans say such coinage "is sure to produce conditions even worse than those from which relief was sought." They boast that "every American dollar is a gold dollar or its equivalent, and American credit stands higher than that of any other nation." At the Democratic Convention in Kansas City, candidate William Jennings Bryan threatens to withdraw if the platform doesn't include a plank calling for unlimited silver coinage. He gets his way, and also becomes again the Democratic candidate. The Democratic platform demands "an American financial system made by the American people for themselves, and which restores and maintains a bi-metallic price level, and as a part of such system, the immediate restoration of the free and unlimited coinage of silver and gold at the present legal ratio of 16 to 1, without waiting for the aid or consent of any other nation." The fusion faction of the Peoples Party platform denounces the Gold Standard Act of March 14, 1900 as "the culmination of a long series of conspiracies to deprive the people of their constitutional rights over the money of the nation." The Peoples Party platform repeats the call for free and unlimited coinage of silver and gold at the present legal ratio of 16 to 1, and demands an immediate increase in the output of silver coins. Coming from states like Colorado which favor the coinage of silver, "Silver Republicans" convene and declare their support for Democratic candidates William Jennings Bryan and the vice-presidential nominee, Adlai E. Stevenson.

<u>October, 1900</u> Fears that the Democratic ticket might win cause "Bryan Days" on Wall Street. The price decline is tempered by the belief of many that the Nebraskan can't win.

<u>November 6, 1900</u> In the elections, McKinley again defeats Bryan, and by a greater margin than before. The Republicans strengthen their control of both houses of Congress. The American public thus shows less concern than four years earlier about Bryan's "cross of gold." Silver is tarnished, but thanks to the farming and ranching, Pitkin County survives.

CHAPTER NINE

THE FAT LADY SINGS

January, 1901 The US Mint estimates world output of silver in 1900 was 179 million ounces, an all time record and up 11.5 million ounces from 1899. Despite the increased output, purchases by the Indian Government cause the silver price to rise from 59.1 cents an ounce in January, 1900 to 66.3 cents an ounce at year end. Is silver coming back for good?

July 4, 1901 The New York Times reports that Jerome B. Wheeler is filing for bankruptcy protection in the US District Court in New York City. The only company it lists as an asset of Wheeler is the Croesus Gold Mining and Milling Company in California. The Times quotes Wheeler's comment that the two failed Colorado banks of which he had been president had paid off their depositors in full, with interest, within one year of their closing. Until 1888, Wheeler was a part owner of the R. H. Macy Company in New York. In Aspen he founded the Wheeler Bank, the Jerome Hotel and the Wheeler Opera House, and was the major owner of the Aspen Mining and Smelting Company. He was a Colorado Midland Railroad investor and director.

July 10, 1901 Twelve men (not including Porter Nelson) incorporate the Grand View Canal and Irrigation Company in Delta County for 20 years. The company will irrigate land south of Hotchkiss, drawing water from Smith's Fork of the Gunnison River and its tributaries. The main office of the company is in Delta, but a branch office is located in Aspen where meetings of the board of directors will be held.

July 30, 1901 J. Henry Nelson buys a 15/24th interest in the Robert E. Lee Lode in the Tin Cup mining district of Gunnison County. Porter Nelson had bought an interest in the same lode in 1891. Julia's seller: T. G. Lyster, the Aspen banker. Between this date and 1910, J.(Julia) Henry appears several more times as a buyer of mines in Gunnison County.

March 13, 1902 William Jennings Bryan visits politicians and newsmen in Washington, acting like a party leader and not a discarded figure. He says the big questions in the coming election will be imperialism, curbing trusts, and finance. He leaves to deliver a speech in Culpeper before returning to Washington for more politics. Porter Nelson sells two Culpeper County land parcels (deed book 33, pages 207 and 426).

August 5, 1902 Porter Nelson buys his last property in Aspen: Lot M, Block 30. He may be doing this as a courtesy to the seller, Ella Stallard, the wife of his old friend from Culpeper, Edgar Stallard. He had bought his last Pitkin County mining property two years earlier, called, appropriately enough, the Last Chance Lode. Nelson's name will appear in Pitkin records after this date, but not as a buyer of property.

November 26, 1902 The price of silver in London and New York hits a record low, 21 7/8 pence and 47 1/4 cents respectively. Experts say the drop is due to silver sales by China to raise money to pay the Boxer Rebellion indemnity.

August, 1903 The miner's union calls for workers all over Colorado to walk out in support of striking mill workers in Colorado City, who are demanding an 8-hour day.

<u>September 5, 1903</u> Despite a threat from a union mobster, Colorado Governor Peabody orders National Guard units to strike-struck Victor in the Cripple Creek mining district, to stop any violence.

<u>November, 1903</u> Governor Peabody orders out more National Guard troops. They go to Telluride where owners are trying to use non-union workers. About 100 mines across Colorado close down, and 10,000 miners are out of work. Decaying Aspen escapes any strike action or violence.

<u>Political conventions, 1904</u> The Republican Convention in Chicago in June nominates Theodore Roosevelt. Their platform praises past Republican administrations for firmly establishing the gold standard over Democratic opposition. The Democratic Convention begins in July in St. Louis and greets Cleveland's name with wild cheering. The Democratic nominee this year, Alton B. Parker, puts an end to Democratic flirtation with silver by declaring the gold standard to be an established fact. Bryan still has influence enough to head off adoption of a plank saying that due to the recent gold discoveries, silver coinage is no longer an important issue. The Peoples Party platform attacks the gold standard and specie payment resumption, proclaiming that "the Constitution gives to Congress alone power to issue money and regulate its value. We therefore demand that all money shall be issued by the Government in such quantity as shall maintain stability in prices, and every dollar shall be full legal tender, none of which shall be a debt redeemable in any other money."

<u>November 8, 1904</u> Republican Theodore Roosevelt decisively defeats Democrat Parker. Republicans enjoy overwhelming

majorities in both houses. Colorado votes Republican again. Will western Democrats now see the silver cause as hopeless?

December 2, 1904 Julia Henry Nelson and Mary Clark jointly purchase 161 acres of land in Delta County, and the rights to the Grand View Canal, the Aspen Ditch (first registered in May, 1900), the Castle Rock Ditch and Reservoir system and other ditches irrigating the 161 acres and adjoining lands. The seller: Aspen attorney Harold Clark, husband of Mary and an Aspen neighbor of the Nelsons. Estate planning?

December 13, 1904 Julia Henry buys lots in the town of Paonia, Delta County. Is Delta now Eden for Aspenites?

July 9, 1905 The New York Times wonders in print why prices are fluctuating much more than called for by changes in the gold supply. It recalls that mines produced $800 million in gold in the first half of the 19th century, and $3.5 billion between 1890 and 1904. In 1903, world gold production in fact was the largest ever. Contrary to theory, world commodity prices didn't rise, but fell by 40%. Inconsistently, the Times then goes on to urge that China and the US totally abandon silver and firmly adopt gold mono-metallism.

October 18, 1905 Times must be good for Porter Nelson. He gives $10 to Julia Henry and to each of his three children. He asks the children to sign a receipt as follows: "Received of W. Porter Nelson ten dollars which I am to invest, and I agree to report to him on the investment, in writing, every six months from this date." Carmer and Kate reply in writing 6 months later that they had not found a suitable investment. Marguerite reports only a year later:

"Received of W. Porter Nelson on October eighteenth, nineteen hundred and five, ten dollars ($10). I put it in a pocketbook and stuck it in a drawer. I thought of doing several things with it, but I did not get around to it. I will try to do better in the next six months." Is he trying to teach his children the time value of money?

Beginning, 1906 The average price for silver bullion in London in 1905 was 27 3/4 pence an ounce (equivalent to 56 US cents), down slightly from the 1905 average. The owners of the Yule Marble Quarry form the Crystal River and San Juan Railroad Company. It plans to build a 7 ½ mile standard gauge rail line to the quarry from the current rail terminus at the Placita coal station above Redstone. J. Henry Nelson buys from M. C. McNichols of Aspen, acting as attorney for Mrs. S. Henney, a 1/8th interest in the Jessie (Twilight) claim in the Quartz Creek gold mining district near Pitkin in Gunnison County. Real estate dealer Andrew McQueen of Aspen notarizes McNichols' signature. Two years later, Julia Henry buys another quarter interest in the claim, with realty broker Amos Bourquin the notary for this deed.

May, 1906 At the first Monday in May election for the board of Pitkin County's School District No. 1 (Aspen), Porter Nelson and Elias Cohn are elected members. Although not active in school affairs before, Nelson is elected Board President. Cohn is chosen to fill out the remaining year of the term of a retiring member. In 1900, young Missouri-born Elias Cohn was just a cashier at an Aspen bank and a new father. He later became bookkeeper for Aspen schools. In 1906, he is David Hyman's chief representative in Aspen, succeeding Samuel I. Hallett.

July, 1906 In London, William Jennings Bryan announces that he continues to support silver and will ignore the Party's current money plank if he is again the nominee. Two weeks later, King Edward receives him in private audience. Republicans hope Bryan continues to make pronouncements, which serve to divide the Democrats. Bryan soon corrects himself, saying in London that the silver question is passe, that if he is the nominee again, he will campaign on three issues: tariff revision, curbing trusts, and Philippine self government. The Aspen Daily Times carries an interview with James Stewart, manager of the North Pole mines near Crystal. He says that he is ready to start up the compressor at the mines, and the Grand Junction smelter is sending teams to haul away ore. The Daily Times urges Aspen citizens to trim trees along the streets, as the "cotton" coming off the trees is a nuisance. The paper on July 20 reports Mrs. Porter Nelson and children are off to Glenwood for some weeks.

August 7, 1906 Amazing news. The War Department has a new system for identifying enlisted men: finger prints.

August 14, 1906 The Aspen Daily Times reports that Porter Nelson, "popular townsman and president of the school board," left on Sunday for Culpeper, Virginia due to the serious illness of his father. His father dies in Culpeper just six days later, age 87, on the same day as Aspen learns of Utes on the rampage near Douglas, Wyoming. They had left their Utah reservation saying they would visit the Sioux in Montana.

August 28, 1906 The Aspen Daily Times notes the return from Glenwood of Mrs. Porter Nelson and children.

September 5, 1906 Silver is 67 1/4 cents an ounce, lead is $5.75 a hundred weight. The Aspen Daily Times reports both Porter Nelson's return from his trip to Virginia caused by his father's illness and death, and his subsequent departure for Crystal. The paper then reports that a dozen Aspen citizens are departing for Goldfield, Nevada to seek their fortunes.

September 13, 1906 Concerned at the outflow of gold, the Bank of England raises its discount rate from 3 1/2% to 4%. Two subsequent increases bring the discount rate up to 6% a month later. The Bank also advises that English firms not extend credits to America, but ask for payment when due.

September 23-30, 1906 Secretary of War William Howard Taft now heads a new American-installed provisional government in Cuba, and US army troops are ready to go there. The US government is buying silver again. Even Mexico is buying silver in the US, to produce needed silver coins. Lasting reason to hope for Aspen silver?

October 2, 1906 The Denver mint is now turning out only silver coins. The Aspen Daily Times reports that the Women's Guild of the Episcopal Church is meeting at 2 PM this afternoon at the home of Mrs. W. Porter Nelson. The paper notes she and Porter are just back from a week in Crystal.

October 5, 1906 The Tri-Counties (Pitkin, Eagle, Garfield) Fair closes. Some Aspenites want it to be an annual event.

October 17-20, 1906 The Treasury says it will now receive bids from would-be silver sellers three times a week. The silver price is 70 cents an ounce, the highest since the repeal of the Sherman Act. Aspen mine owners announce that they will put into force as of November 1 the wage scale they had agreed in 1893 to pay if silver ever reached 83 cents an ounce. This increases miners' wages from $2.25 a day to $2.75. The Aspen High football team defeats the Leadville team 62-0, in a snow storm.

October 31, 1906 The Aspen Democrat notes the phenomenal growth of the Post Office in Goldfield, Nevada. Its turnover now is on a par with Salt Lake City, Oakland, or Springfield, Ohio. The paper reports that several Aspenites who recently went to the Nevada gold fields have all found good jobs. It says also that several deaths resulted from fights between persons jostling to be in a good position when the government opens the Walker Indian reservation in Nevada. The Utes from the Utah reservation who are now in Wyoming are said to be "on the warpath," with the 10th Cavalry in pursuit.

November 3, 1906 Word reaches Aspen that the Utes have decided to abandon the warpath. Chiefs Black Whiskers and Redtop instead will go to Washington to arbitrate the Indians' grievances. The heirs of Lewis Porter Nelson enter into the property records of Culpeper County, Va. (deed book 38, page 115) their agreement on the division of his estate. The estate consists primarily of real property valued at over $120,000. The heirs drew lots to decide who will receive the seven portions of almost equal value into which the estate is divided. Porter Nelson drew two lots, one for himself and his children, and one for the heirs of his older half-brother, Lucian. Several of Lucian's heirs live in Pueblo, Colorado.

November 6, 1906 Republicans win most state offices in Colorado, and some even in normally Democratic Pitkin County. Aspen cigar and liquor store owner Henry Beck, a Republican, becomes the area's new state representative.

November 9-20, 1906 Theodore Roosevelt is travelling by warship to Panama. When he lands, he becomes the first serving American President ever to set foot on foreign soil. The Director of US Mint predicts the silver price will rise above the present 71 cents an ounce. He says the Mint will not play games but will continue to buy the 7 to 10 million ounces of silver a year it needs. Three days later, the Treasury makes him a bad prophet by suspending silver purchases because of the high price. The American Federation of Labor comes out in favor of allowing women to vote. The chimney of Aspen's Holden Works is taken down, and the bricks shipped away. Many townspeople turn out to see some long time Aspen residents leave for the Nevada gold fields. D. R. C. Brown's Castle Creek Water Company offers to reduce household water bills in Aspen from $24 to $17.50 a year, in return for a new 20 year franchise. The school board, presided over by President Nelson, considers imposing a $4 a month charge for children of non-residents attending high school, and $2 for grade school. These fees are to cover 80% of the cost of schooling one child. The Aspen Democrat reports that Lewis Nelson, who has been in Aspen visiting his brother Porter, is returning to Virginia. Porter Nelson's house at 525 West Hallam (along with hundreds of properties of other owners) is advertised for a tax sale on December 12. Nelson owes some $30 in unpaid 1905 taxes on the house.

November 21-30, 1906 The Democrat reports that the Colorado Fuel and Iron Company, in which Redstone's John Osgood is a leading figure, is planning to build a tramway and rail line at Ashcroft, the "Paradise of the Elk Mountains," to exploit the iron ore there. The Castle Creek Water Company rejects Aspen's demand for a 30% reduction in rates. It counteroffers to reduce rates by 27 1/2% and forgive city debts up to January 1, 1906, in return for a new 25 year franchise and a city levy of 3 mills to pay future water bills. The Democrat sneers that this would still leave Aspen water rates double those of Leadville. The council decides to call a special election for the citizens to vote on the question. On the cheery side, the paper says that Denver millionaire James F. Burns is moving to Goldfield, Nevada and will start a railroad there. Goldfield's hot. The Wheeler Opera House puts on a show about Goldfield; general admission, 50 cents.

December 1-22, 1906 The Democrat reports that the Guggenheim's American Smelting and Refining Company is offering a record high price for lead, $6.00 a hundred pounds. Also that the Army is sending two regiments to Hawaii because of fears that Japan might invade the island of Lanai. A few days later, the paper headlines: "Soundings of Monterey Bay by Innocent-Looking Japanese Fishermen. Santa Cruz an Ideal Spot for the Landing of a Hostile Army." Must Aspen worry about this, too? Miners go out on strike in Goldfield, Nevada. The Aspen Daily Times notes that Mr. and Mrs. Porter Nelson are leaving for an extended vacation in the East. Three weeks later the paper reports Porter back in Aspen to take the children to Denver for the holidays to join Mrs. Nelson. She had stayed there on returning from the East.

December 27, 1906 Aspen learns details of the proposed grant of a new franchise to the Castle Creek Water Company. Aspen voters are to accept or reject the proposed franchise in a special election on February 5, 1907.

December 31, 1906 J. Henry Nelson, and the Raymond Consolidated Mines Co., receive a US patent to the Jessie Lode mining claim in Gunnison County. The patent bears the signature of President Theodore Roosevelt. Julia Henry apparently has no fear of the suspicion-arousing name for the mining district in which the lode is located: Gold Brick.

January 8, 1907 The Aspen Daily Times reports that Carmer Nelson is leaving for Denver to join his mother and sisters for the rest of the winter. She and the children actually end up in California. Does Julia Henry find Aspen hard to take?

January 27, 1907 Nevada gold mining seems to attract many these days. After a week looking at mines in Goldfield, Nevada, D. R. C. Brown returns to Denver. The Rio Grande advertises "Spend your winter on the Pacific Coast," something Julia Henry and the children are already doing.

January 29, 1907 The Aspen Daily Times publishes a report by Colonel Ed F. Browne giving a favorable assessment of mining prospects in Nevada south of Tonopah. But a week later, the paper urges Aspen "to stop the Nevada exodus."

February 1-20, 1907 The option expires for the dam site on the Roaring Fork River. Aspen voters approve the new franchise for the Castle Creek Water Company. New Aspen State Representative Henry Beck introduces a bill in the

General Assembly calling for Gunnison County Commissioners to submit to a vote the question of ceding to Pitkin County the Marble-Crystal area, which is cut off by high mountains from the rest of Gunnison County. Several Aspenites who left for Goldfield, Nevada reportedly are coming back.

February 26, 1907 Porter Nelson buys all interest in the Lucky Boy mine on Sheep Mountain near Crystal in Gunnison County. The seller is Nelson's old Aspen friend, Ed Ogden.

March 5-12, 1907 Congress closes its session, having appropriated the prodigious amount of $1 billion! Julia Henry and children are away from Aspen in warm Southern California, Porter Nelson is away in Nevada. The Aspen Daily Times reports that he and James Stewart now are prospecting some miles east of Goldfield, Nevada. Also, former Aspenite Raymond Thayer is the proud owner of the Oro Assay office in Goldfield, and former Aspenite P. J. Harrington is managing a large mine there.

March 13-29, 1907 The Aspen Daily Times reports panic on Wall Street, which has brought Northern Pacific shares to their lowest level in 6 years, and Union Pacific shares at their lowest level in 10 years. With financiers begging for money, Treasury Secretary Cortelyou orders that Customs receipts be deposited in New York banks. The Aspen Daily Times reports receipt of a letter from Mrs. Porter Nelson from Santa Barbara, California saying that she and the children will return to Aspen when school is out. The Times also says that Porter Nelson and James Stewart, prospecting in Nevada for some weeks, are now near Buckskin. They will be coming home soon. No word on what if anything they found.

April 1-15, 1907 The New York Times again discusses the odd action of prices under the gold standard. It says that prices have not conformed to the theory that gold supply is the major determinant of price movements. Price levels fell between 1886 and 1896 when gold output doubled, but prices then rose 30% between 1896 and 1906 as gold output doubled again. The Times says this might provide a new theoretical basis for supporters of bi-metallism in England and on the Continent. Analysts ascribe the recent sharp drop in the London silver price to 30 pence an ounce to heavy Chinese selling to pay its debts to Europe. The Colorado General Assembly approves the bill submitted by Aspen delegate Henry Beck calling for a vote on the cession to Pitkin County of the Marble-Crystal area in Gunnison County. The Aspen Daily Times reports the return of Porter Nelson from Nevada for the annual meeting of the School Board, of which he is President. Aspen schools have 353 male, 402 female students.

April 18-28, 1907 Porter Nelson and W. S. Copeland, describing themselves as "two legal voters," publish a notice in the Aspen Daily Times that the Aspen school board will hold a meeting at 1:45 PM on May 6 at Lincoln School for the purpose of electing one new board member. No election could be held at the annual meeting due to lack of advance notice. The Times recalls that a year ago when two vacancies needed filling, two able men came forward: W. P. Nelson and Elias Cohn. Both were elected unanimously, Cohn to fill out the last year of a retiring member. The Times says two persons now are offering their candidacies for the school board vacancy: Cohn and Charles Moore. With the Aspen school board weighing establishing a Manual Training Department and a Domestic Science Department, the Times argues that Mr. Cohn is more likely to push these proposals successfully.

May 21- June 2, 1907 Aspen's new school board meets and elects Elias Cohn President. School districts other than Aspen vote to add a small levy to support Aspen High School, which in exchange will not charge out-of-district students a tuition fee. The High School thus serves not just the city.

May 26-30, 1907 In New York, David Hyman and D. R. C. Brown reach an amicable settlement of their dispute over the "Georgia" or "Boomerang" fraction on Aspen Mountain. The Aspen Daily Times says that Alderman J. B. Switzer and forester I. W. Foster are back from a trip to Hotchkiss and Paonia, with good things to say about that area. Also, two recent cases of scarlet fever in Aspen prove to be of the most malignant type. City physician Dr. Twining, Father Servant, the school board and Aspen school superintendent Lanning meet to decide what preventive steps to take.

June 2, 1907 Porter Nelson formally steps down as School Board President in favor of Elias Cohn. The Aspen Democrat says Nelson leaves "with the respect of every member of the Board and the admiration of every patron of the schools. During the past year, Mr. Nelson has been a tireless worker for the advancement and uplifting of our schools, and he has been a fair and impartial officer."

June 12, 1907 The Democrat reports that the Callahan shaft in Tourtelotte Park is now shipping ore. Aspen store owner Henry Beck, a major shareholder, says that the mine will soon top the list of Aspen mines paying dividends. That list is a very short one, but let's keep hope alive.

June 21, 1907 The Democrat publishes a letter from the Miners Union in Goldfield, Nevada: "Advise all miners and laborers to stay away from Goldfield. More men than jobs."

July 1, 1907 A revised mining law comes into effect in Nevada. The Democrat asserts that more Eastern money will soon be coming into Pitkin County, especially Tourtelotte Park and Richmond Hill, from Chicago. Back home, Carmer praises his father, now in Santa Barabara, for "fine housekeeping."

July 16, 1907 The Chicago Mining, Milling and Development Company starts work on six claims in Queens Gulch. The Democrat reports Porter Nelson's return from Santa Barbara.

July 31-August 2, 1907 Scarlet fever is scaring Aspen again; the city bans children from public gatherings. But cheer up, Aspen! B. Clark Wheeler is back in town, saying that within a year, he will have 1,000 men working in the Famous Tunnel on Richmond Hill! Also, L. A. W. Brown is sprucing up his office in the Aspen Block. The Acting Comptroller of the Currency issues order number 8815 allowing the new Peoples National Bank in Aspen to begin operations. An easterner leases the premises of the former J. B. Wheeler bank for the new bank's operations.

September 15, 1907 The Aspen City Council publishes its ordinance extending the franchise of the Castle Creek Water Company of West Virginia for 25 years until October 31, 1930. The terms are as in the original franchise of 1885.

September-October 5, 1907 The Democrat gives front page coverage to this year's Tri-Counties (Pitkin, Eagle, Garfield) Fair in Aspen. Fair backers build the Crystal Palace, the largest exhibit building on the Western Slope. The paper complains that where vacant buildings have been torn down in Aspen, streets are littered with bent and rusty nails. It calls for a moratorium on building demolition until after the Fair. Mayor Cain proclaims the afternoon of October 3 a holiday so all Aspenites can attend the Fair. On that day, the Midland and the Crystal River Railroads run a special train for Fair goers from Marble and Redstone, and some 2,000 persons attend. Redstone's capitalist, John C. Osgood, gives the Fair strong backing. Mrs. Osgood wins a prize for being the best lady driver of a span of horses. Mrs. S. I. Hallett wins a prize for having the best horse.

October 11, 1907 The Aspen Post Office gets the latest technology: a stamp cancelling machine. Letters are now cancelled by turning a crank. The Democrat reports that Dr. Guthrie is back in Aspen after visiting his family in Boulder. Dr. Guthrie keeps his office in the Aspen Block.

October 16, 1907 When banks open in Goldfield, Nevada, crowds of depositors demand their money. The panic stops when someone ostentatiously deposits $50,000 in gold coin.

October 18-23, 1907 The New York Clearing House demands that all directors of the Mercantile Bank resign, as a condition of aiding that troubled bank. The Knickerbocker Trust in New York closes its doors. All over the country, depositors panic and rush to withdraw money from bank accounts. The interest rate for call money in New York jumps to 10%. The New

York Clearing House tries to project confidence by announcing that it will aid any member bank hit by a run. John D. Rockefeller and J. P. Morgan pledge support for the banks. The next day, the Treasury deposits $25 million in New York banks to show confidence in their soundness.

October 24, 1907 The Democrat reports that Harriman is facing ruin, and that all New York state is crippled by the Wall Street panic. A former Aspen resident writes from Goldfield to say that he is leaving there for South Africa.

October 25-28, 1907 Six banks in Brooklyn close their doors. The interest rate skyrockets on call money, when available at all. The New York Clearing House denies that it will resort to issuing certificates instead of cash as it had done in 1893. But a few days later, the Clearing House does do just that when depositors make withdrawals. Similar organizations in other major cities follow suit. Denver's Rocky Mountain News asserts, prematurely, that the financial situation in New York is righting itself and the public is regaining confidence. Later, the News claims Western banks are independent of Wall Street, that there's no reason for the West to be affected. The News opines that New York banks' issuance of "paper money" will calm the panic. The Governor of Oklahoma declares a legal holiday. Governors in Nevada, California and Oregon follow suit. Banks in those states suspend payments of cash. The big banks forming the Denver Clearing House adopt the practice of eastern cities, and begin giving out certificates instead of cash. Denver banks issue up to $1 million of such certificates, in denominations of $5, $10 and $20, backed by good collateral worth at least 1/3 more than the face value of the certificates. Banks in other cities like Colorado

Springs also issue certificates instead of cash, but banks in such smaller places as Aspen, Leadville and Canyon City continue to pay out cash.

<u>November 1, 1907</u> The interest rate on call money in New York drops from 75% to 20%, suggesting that the crisis is easing somewhat. Former silver champion William Jennings Bryan says in Omaha that crisis cannot last long, the US being such a large gold (yes, gold) producer. The Colorado state game and fish warden says he will ensure that Utes from Utah don't come into western Colorado again to hunt.

<u>November 3, 1907</u> New York Clearing House banks are almost $40 million short of the amount needed to meet all their obligations to corresponding banks throughout the country. Seventeen big bankers meet there on what to do about the crisis. In an effort to calm the panic, the steamer Lusitania is rushing $10 million in British gold to New York.

<u>November 5-7, 1907</u> In the midst of the financial crisis on Wall Street, B. Clark Wheeler sends word to Aspen from New York that he has obtained financing for expanding the Famous tunnel. One thing he undoubtedly uses to get the money is a July 29, 1907 to-whom-it-may-concern letter. In it, scores of Aspen leaders endorse the soundness of the project; D. R. C. Brown's name tops the list of signers. W. Porter Nelson signs as a "mining expert." In Denver, the Carpenters Union advises its members to accept Clearing House certificates instead of cash. Some big mining companies draw gold coins from the Denver Mint to pay their workers. The Treasury tells that mint to ship to Chicago 30 tons of silver coins, half dollars and quarters. A former Aspenite,

George Thatcher, who went to Nevada thirty months ago, returns to tell the Aspen Democrat of the many valuable mining properties he now controls in Rhyolite, Goldfield, Manhattan, Tonopah and Round Mountain, Nevada.

November 8, 1907 To stem the gold outflow, the Bank of England raises its discount rate to 7%, a level not seen since the 1873 Panic. The Lusitania arrives in New York with its $10 million in gold, having made the crossing in the record time of 115 hours. The Treasury tries to restore confidence by depositing public monies in some banks in the South and West. Former Aspenite Mrs. Neipur writes back from Cherry Creek, Nevada, saying that she is disappointed there, that Mr. Neipur lost his job in the crash. They are returning to Aspen.

November 8-12, 1907 The Aspen Democrat reports that people in Denver are readily accepting cashiers checks issued by local banks. Aspen still has plenty of currency to meet payrolls. The paper hails the visit of Chicago capitalists to Richmond Hill mining properties and the Famous tunnel. The ladies of St. Mary's Catholic Church postpone a scheduled fair because of Aspen's latest scarlet fever epidemic.

November 17, 1907 In New York, the President of the Knickerbocker Trust Company when it went bankrupt, Charles T. Barney, commits suicide. In Aspen, City Physician Dr. W. H. Twining agrees that sprinkling the streets of Aspen to lay dust could help combat the scarlet fever contagion. The Castle Creek Water Company agrees to supply water for this purpose without charge to the city, although water levels in Castle Creek are always low at this time of year.

November 19, 1907 Daniel Guggenheim, President of the American Smelting and Refining Company, says the company is going flat out to meet the Government's call for maximum output of gold and silver bullion. In Aspen, the long list of properties on which 1906 taxes have not been paid includes, as did last year's list, the three lots in block 29, valued at $215, on which the Nelson house stands. Nelson again has good company on the delinquent list: e. g. Edgar Stallard, B. Clark Wheeler, his Aspen Consolidated Mining Company, the Mollie Gibson mine, Aspen Mining and Smelting company.

November 21, 1907 Mayor Cain says that, to combat scarlet fever, the Aspen Fire Department will be back out sprinkling the city streets, helping the regular sprinkler wagon. Priority will be given to sprinkling streets around schools. David Hyman's Smuggler mine closes "for repairs."

November-December, 1907 On November 20, three large New York banks (J. P. Morgan, First National and National City) announce, as a confidence building gesture, that they will pay hard money to buy up $25 million in Clearing House certificates. In the latter part of November, J. P. Morgan persuades the Bank of France to send $60 million in gold to New York, further bolstering confidence in US banks. Call money in New York now costs "only" 11%. Washington tells the Denver Mint to turn out only silver coins as of December 1; the mint can produce $80,000 such coins a day. In his State of Union message to the Congress in early December, President Theodore Roosevelt calls on citizens to stop hoarding and deposit their money in sound banks. He also proposes establishment of a Bureau of Mines, a step welcomed by the Aspen Democrat. The paper reports train trips by Porter

Nelson to Carbondale and to Crystal. When he was younger, Nelson often made such trips by bicycle. Not now.

December 11, 1907 Silver is now 55 ½ cents an ounce, lead 3.85 cents a pound, eggs 30 cents a dozen, butter 3 pounds for $1. The Democrat reports that three former Aspen residents are doing well who recently took up homesteads on former Indian reservation lands in Idaho.

December 13, 1907 City-County Physician H. W. Twining attacks rumors that young Aspenites attending college will not be allowed to return home for the holidays, due to alleged rampant disease in Aspen. Twining says public health in Aspen is no worse than elsewhere in Colorado.

December 19, 1907 The assessed value of property in Pitkin County is $2,284,000 in 1907, up slightly from 1906. Mrs. S. I. Hallett leaves Aspen for Chihuahua, Mexico, where her husband is managing a large mine. The Halletts will tour South America before she returns to Aspen in the summer.

December 21, 1907 David Hyman keeps the pumps going in his Smuggler and Durant mines to prevent flooding. The Democrat says owner Hyman, company President Charles Hughes and local manager Elias Cohn closed the mines only reluctantly, and hope that metal prices will recover soon so the mines can reopen. The paper says that the failure of Westinghouse Electric, which helped drive down the price of copper, also hurt lead and zinc prices. Still, it asserts that "Aspen is the last city in the West to feel the effects of the financial storm which has swept the country in the last two months . . . The darkest hour is just before the dawn . . . Smile and push!"

December 22-31, 1907 Silver is 52 ½ cents an ounce. The Democrat hopes that some mine owners will now reduce their royalties, enabling more miners to lease workings. The owners of the Argentium-Juniata say they will cut their royalty demands as of January 1, 1908. Colorado's junior Senator, Simon Guggenheim, says that depressed conditions in silver countries India and China caused the US silver price to fall.

January, 1908 A French historian predicts that Japan will soon attack the US fleet. Call (overnight) money still costs 15% in New York, while sixty day money costs only 12%. This suggests lenders expect the money squeeze to ease further. Banks stop issuing certificates and resume cash payments. The 1907 panic, if short, was more severe than the panic of 1893. In the latter panic, the nation's banks issued only $69 million of certificates instead of cash vs. over $250 million in 1907. William Jennings Bryan in a Nacogdoches, Texas speech announces that he will again run for President.

January 14-15, 1908 In Washington, Treasury Secretary Cortelyou denies that he will resign to become President of the failed Knickerbocker Trust Company. Aspen Mayor Cain and School Board Chairman Elias Cohn appear before the Pitkin County Board of Commissioners to ask that county quarantine officers be kept on duty until the scarlet fever epidemic is over. Judge Shumate urges the Board to appoint an outside accountant to study the county's books for alleged skulduggery. Some years before, a panel comprised of C. F. Brown of the Roaring Fork Electric Company, and the accountants of the Mollie Gibson and Smuggler Mines had examined County books for another suspected malfeasance.

January 18-31, 1908 The New York Clearing House reports an increase in recent weeks of $27 million in hard cash held by its members. By the end of January, New York interest rates are back at pre-crisis levels: call money is 2% and 60 days money is 4%. The crisis may be over, but anyone living on short term credits (Porter Nelson?) from mid-October to mid-January has gone through the wringer. In Aspen, David Hyman's manager, Elias Cohn, denies rumors that Hyman and the Guggenheim group are about to buy out the local properties of D. R. C. Brown. To save money, Aspen cuts salaries and positions, turns off lights, etc. The number of lights in city hall drops to 20 from 38, and 26 street lights go dark. The Rio Grande and the Midland railroads reduce tariffs for hauling coal into Aspen by 50 cents a ton. The Democrat says "with cheaper coal and reduced royalties, truly the people of Aspen have things to be thankful for."

February 3-5, 1908 The Democrat reports that Mr. and Mrs. W. Porter Nelson will give a dinner for the Episcopal Bishop for Western Colorado, Bishop Knight. The Bishop, from Glenwood Springs, is to hold a service at Christ Episcopal Church. He probably approves at this time the removal of St. John's Chapel from declining Aspen and its shipment to growing Marble. The coke ovens at Cardiff close. The Italian coke makers who worked there move on to other places. Aspen's school superintendent invites the public to attend a variety show being staged, at the Wheeler Opera House, by 45 Aspen High School students seeking to raise money to buy a set of encyclopedias for the school.

February 6, 1908 The Democrat crows that the Democratic Pitkin County commissioners are forcing the County to hire W. Porter Nelson, helped by Arthur W. Hull, to audit the County books covering the past six years. Nelson and Hull will be paid $10 a day, for a total not to exceed $1,250. The Aspen Daily times attacks this choice, charging that Nelson has not paid taxes on his home since 1897 while his children are being educated at County expense, that he is not an accountant, and that no one has heard of him keeping even a day book. It further charges that Nelson owes money to many persons, and is beholden to some of the persons whose activities are the subject of the investigation.

February 7, 1908 The Democrat defends Nelson against the attack by the Aspen Daily Times. The Democrat says: "Mr. Nelson has given his fortune to Colorado. He came here while times were still prosperous, before the Republicans, together with Wall Street sharks, `benevolently assimilated' and robbed silver of its value. He purchased the Aspen Block, paying $45,000. The commercial value of the block went rapidly to the bad. He has brought into Pitkin and Gunnison counties more than $250,000 of Eastern capital, to be expended among merchants and miners. He is a graduate civil engineer of one of the great colleges of the United States, and has worked behind the transit on very difficult and important work. To say that he is not an accountant is to say that the party making such a statement is either utterly ignorant or prejudiced, and to say the least, utterly unreliable. Above all, W. Porter Nelson is a gentleman and will not vary from the truth one iota." Roanoke College no doubt is pleased by the Democrat's label for it. "Behind the transit" refers to Nelson's work for the Santa Fe Railroad.

THE FAT LADY SINGS

February 8, 1908 Dudley Tollman, a partner in Brown and Tollman, Assayers and Mining Engineers, closes his office in Aspen to move to Searchlight, Nevada. He has done much work for the Smuggler mine. A sample of low grade Aspen silver ore is sent to Nevada where the largest cyanide mill operating in the US will test processing it there.

February 11, 1908 The Democrat headlines: "County Clerk Turns Over Game Money. Experts Nelson and Hull are Doing Excellent Work. The People Will Receive Much Benefit from the Work of These Gentlemen." The term `game money' here means the fees paid for hunting and fishing licenses. The County Clerk, Republican Moses Bradshaw, says that he put the money into the treasury on time, but the Democrat asserts that only the audit forced him to come clean.

February 15, 1908 In Washington, the House Coinage Committee ignores President Theodore Roosevelt and votes out a bill to restore the words "In God We Trust" to gold and silver coins. The silver price is 56 ½ cents an ounce. The Durant hires a few miners to work on its lease of the Spar Consolidated mine on Aspen mountain.

February 22, 1908 The Democrat boasts that Aspen's Peoples National Bank is as sound as any bank in Colorado, and that no Aspen bank failed to meet demands during the crisis.

March 1, 1908 Dunbar Wright, owner of the Mineral Farm property near Aspen, opens it to leasing for the first time.

March 5-11, 1908 The Democrat reports, first, the arrival of B. Clark Wheeler in town for a stay of some time to see about reopening his Famous tunnel. The next day, the paper reports Wheeler's departure for Rawhide, Nevada, which Wheeler claims will become the mining center of that state (actually, the gold of Rawhide peters out in a few years). The Democrat trumpets: "There is good in Aspen," referring to a gold vein found in the Smuggler mine assaying $6-$10 a ton. Skeptics might say that the Smuggler report reflects an attempt to boost the price of its shares. "Smile and Push," the Democrat urges. Note: Aspen grasps now at gold, not silver.

March 15, 1908 Breaking with its usual reporting of alarming stories about gold leaving the United States, the New York Times brags that gold stocks in the United States are over $1 billion. It calls this the "greatest accumulation of the precious metal ever known to history." It says that gold coins owned by the US Government, if sold, would pay off the national debt and leave a goodly sum for other purposes. The US now holds the most gold, with Germany a close second and France third. On a per capita basis, France is the leading gold holder, with $23.57 per Frenchman. The US is second, with $18.66 per American; Germany is third, with $17 per German. The Democrat reports a new mill will be built at Marble the coming summer. The 1908 Aspen telephone directory shows the Nelson family living at 525 West Hallam.

March 17, 1908 Over 2,000 shop workers of the Rio Grande Railroad go out on strike. The Democrat brags that the Aspen State Bank, successor to the First National Bank founded in 1887, met all demands during the panic. D. H. Moffat, Denver's Judge Hallet, and David Hyman control that bank. T. G. Lyster is cashier. A Comptroller of the Currency examiner closes the new Peoples National Bank of Aspen.

<u>March 25, 1908</u> The Aspen City Council debates giving up the horses of the Fire Department, and basing the fire apparatus at a private livery stable. The <u>Democrat</u> opposes this economy plan, fearing fire protection will be weakened.

<u>March 29-30, 1908</u> In Washington, the Senate passes the Aldrich bill. The bill authorizes the Secretary of Treasury in a crisis to issue $500,000,000 in currency to national banks. These in exchange would surrender state, county and municipal bonds as security. In Aspen, the Peoples National Bank reopens. New local owners putting up $25,000 in capital include Mayor (and grocer) Walter G. Cain, clothing store owner Benjamin Kobey, and attorney Harold W. Clark.

<u>April 2, 1908</u> Elias Cohn, manager of the Smuggler and Durant mines, publishes an offer to reopen those mines, if miners will accept the $2.50 a day wage paid in 1906. Some 65 miners show up for work. The Chicago Mining and Development Company is planning to open its operations on Richmond Hill by June 1. Why this renewed interest in silver, when silver is only 55 cents an ounce in New York?

<u>April 6, 1908</u> The <u>Rocky Mountain News</u> lead editorial, keyed to William Jennings Bryan's visit to Colorado, begins "Greetings to the Next President." Colorado still likes Bryan, but the <u>News</u> concedes "the silver question has simply been buried in the golden flood from the mines of the world."

<u>April 7, 1908</u> The Board of Commissioners of Pitkin County meets in all day session to receive a report from W. Porter Nelson and Arthur Hull on their examination of County books for the years 1906, 1905 and part of 1904. The Board decides

to end their auditing contract immediately, and votes to pay them $521.50 for their work to date. The Aspen Daily Times charges that Nelson and Hull only messed around with tax lists, and did not look at other important matters such as county bonds. On the lighter side, boys at Aspen High School go out on strike in the mistaken belief that the faculty is trying to prevent them from walking on the street with girls. The Daily Times opines that the strikers will go back to school when they become convinced the faculty only wants them to concentrate more on their books.

April 20, 1908 Pitkin County Commissioners turn over to the District Attorney for the 9th judicial district, for appropriate action, the report of auditors Nelson and Hull on Pitkin County accounts for 1906 and 1907.

April 23-24, 1908 The apricot trees at Emma are in full bloom. The Democrat: "The Smuggler Mining and Milling Company now employs 275 men. It would be well for Aspen if other mine owners had the pluck of the Smuggler Company." It also reports that "great hustler" B. Clark Wheeler holds 10 gold mining claims in Rawhide, Nevada.

April 30, 1908 In Washington, the House Banking and Currency Committee turns down the Aldrich bill allowing emergency issuance of currency. The Democrat says D. R. C. Brown is preparing the former Hallam Avenue residence of banker T. G. Lyster as a summer home for his family.

May 5-7, 1908 A late cold snap destroys up to 75% of the peach crop in areas like Fruita. The Mountain Ranger mine on Richmond Hill may put in a second shift. The Democrat publishes correspondence from County Attorney Hays and District Attorney Gentry on the Nelson-Hull audit of allegedly deficient Pitkin County accounts.

May 10, 1908 The Democrat prods the Pitkin County Commissioners to look into the question of supposedly missing school funds. Aspen's School Superintendent informs the School Board that he is leaving for Globe, Arizona. The paper also carries the first appearance of a notice filed by W. Porter Nelson of a coming special meeting of the stockholders of the North Pole Mining Company to discuss reorganization.

May 14, 1908 Former County Treasurer W. H. McNichols, whose supposed misdeeds led to demands for an audit of Pitkin County books, asks that the audit be resumed. He agrees to pay some expenses of the audit. The Pitkin County Board then asks Nelson and Hull to resume checking County records, and to go back to January 1, 1903. These two agree to a new contract paying $10 a day, for up to 87 days.

May 16-17, 1908 Well-to-do Pitkin County rancher Fred Light loses a suit to have Agriculture Department regulations limiting grazing in national forests declared unconstitutional. Twenty marble cutters from Vermont arrive to work at the Yule Marble Quarry in Marble.

May 27, 1908 Mrs. Samuel I. Hallett returns to her home in Aspen, much improved in health and spirits after a long stay in Mexico with her husband Samuel, who will come to Aspen later. The Democrat notes that Porter Nelson is off to Crystal to look after his mining properties there.

<u>May 29, 1908</u> Porter Nelson returns from Crystal with a New York expert who was inspecting mines there. Even before she graduates from Aspen High School, Nelson's daughter Kate, of the class of 1908, is elected First Vice President of the Aspen High Alumni Association.

<u>June 1-2, 1908</u> Porter Nelson is chosen as one of Aspen's 4th Precinct delegates to the Pitkin County Democratic Convention in Glenwood Springs that will select delegates to the state Democratic Convention. In a gesture termed "generous" by the <u>Democrat</u>, D. R. C. Brown offers to cut Roaring Fork Electric Company rates in return for a new 20-year franchise. The next day, the <u>Democrat</u> says it would be nice to have all city arc lights back on again. Carmer Nelson plays Mose, the football hero, in the Aspen High class play at the Wheeler Opera House.

<u>June 5-11, 1908</u> The Aspen City Council debates giving the Roaring Fork Electric Company a new franchise. Samples of the new lower rates: 10 cents per KWH if metered. Otherwise a household pays $2 a month for five 16 candle-power incandescent lamps. The city pays $7.50 a month for an all-night arc lamp, or $5 for a light turned out at 10 P.M.. Aspen High graduation ceremonies are held at the Wheeler Opera House. The class, numbering 21, is the second largest in school history. Kate Nelson is the top ranking student, class historian and valedictorian. School Board President Elias Cohn notes that she has won two scholarships: to the University at Boulder, and to Denver University. Several days later, it comes out that Carmer Nelson, 17th in the class, wins a Denver University scholarship.

June 20, 1908 To boost the city, Aspen women take the lead in staging a strawberry shortcake festival at the Fair Grounds, combined with a band concert, a baseball game and ending with a dance. Over 2,500 persons turn out. Mrs. Arthur Hull, responsible for the strawberry part, says that not one of the 453 shortcakes donated by Aspen women was bad! The Aspen baseball team beats arch-rival Leadville, 13-1.

June 24-25, 1908 The Democrat urges Aspen to celebrate a "Trout Day" to bring in fisherman from other places and boost the town. It says "we have fine fishing streams with lots of fish." The Aspen City Council votes unanimously to grant a 20-year franchise to the Roaring Fork Electric Co.

Political conventions, 1908 The Republicans convene in Chicago and nominate William Howard Taft of Ohio. Their platform again endorses the gold standard. Presaging the creation of the Federal Reserve, their platform praises the actions of the Republican administration and Congress in adopting emergency measures to increase liquidity during the Panic of 1907. The Platform goes on: "The Republican party is committed to the development of a permanent currency system, responding to our greater needs . . . The new system must be automatic in operation, minimizing the fluctuations in interest rates, and above all . . . every dollar should be based upon, and as good as, gold." The Democrats for the first time meet in a "Western" city, Denver. The old nemesis of Colorado silverites, Grover Cleveland, dies just before the Democratic Convention opens. To heal wounds, the convention adjourns for one day in his honor. The Democrats nominate Bryan again, but there is no free silver language in the platform. The platform speaks of a new "emergency currency to be issued by the Federal Government." This currency can be "loaned on adequate security to National and State Banks." The 1908 Peoples Party platform contains language like that of 1904: the issuance of money should not be delegated to any "corporation or individual" (or bank clearing house?).

July 3, 1908 Washington experts sent to audit the Denver Mint count $50 million in gold coins and $10 million in silver dollars, before adjourning for the July 4 holiday. The Hallam Land Company deeds its holdings around Hallam Lake to Pitkin County and Aspen.

July 6, 1908 Porter Nelson and Arthur Hull file the final report on their audit of Pitkin County records. The County thanks Nelson and Hull for their work. Ex-Treasurer McNichols is expected to make good any shortfall found.

July 9, 1908 The Roaring Fork Electric Company puts a large converter on display in front of the Cowenhoven Building. The device will be used at the Castle Creek plant. When it is in operation, the Roaring Fork plant can be idled.

July 11, 1908 Aspen Mayor Cain declares July 16 a city holiday so that all city residents can go to Redstone for a picnic organized by the Methodist Church. The Osgood coal interests in Redstone are ready to welcome the Aspen contingent, and the railroad sets a bargain round trip fare of $1.75 per adult, 90 cents per child. As always in these times, Redstone and Aspen work to develop their ties.

July 16, 1908 The Democrat predicts that a thousand Aspenites will go to Redstone, with 10 coaches available to handle the picnic goers. Actually, 500 make it to Redstone; 100 then go on to Marble to inspect marble quarry operations.

July 23, 1908 D. R. C. Brown and others form a new State Bank of Aspen to take over the old Aspen State Bank. Its capital is $25,000, like the competing Peoples National Bank in which several prominent Aspen Democrats are involved.

July 29, 1908 William H. McNichols, the former Pitkin County Treasurer, is arrested on charges of misappropriating County money. A week later, he appears in court with his lawyer, and offers to pay most of the deficient amount, plus half the cost of the audit. The County Commissioners, after some debate, vote 2-1 to accept the offer.

August 12-19, 1908 The price of silver bullion drops to 51 3/8 cents an ounce. Feeling a financial pinch, Porter Nelson sends his family east. They will visit, first, Julia Henry Nelson's mother in Baltimore, and then his many relatives in Culpeper. His well-to-do sister, Lucille Miller, invites Julia Henry and her two daughters to stay on with her in Virginia. Carmer suggests to his father that he not attend college in the fall, but go to work to ease the burden on family finances. Lucille Miller's husband, Clifford, proposes that the Aspen Nelsons move to Richmond, where Clifford is ready to help Porter buy a part interest in a small company. But Porter hesitates to give up his Colorado dreams.

August 20, 1908 Silver sinks to the lowest price since 1903, 51 1/8 cents an ounce. In Aspen, the Hotel Jerome reopens under new, local management. Don't give up the ship!

August 23, 1908 The Commissioners of Pitkin county meet in a special session to consider the proposal of John Osgood to build a road between Carbondale and Redstone. Much of proposed road would run through Pitkin territory. The road would use part of an old Elk Mountain and Aspen Western Railroad right of way. The Commissioners also consider a proposal that Pitkin County now take steps to annex the portion of Gunnison County around Marble and Crystal as envisaged in the bill state representative Henry Beck sponsored in 1907. The annexation proposal put before the Commissioners calls for circulating a petition to put the question on the ballot in Pitkin and Gunnison Counties at the November election. T. M. Gibb of Redstone undertakes to secure the necessary signatures. Appearing before the Board on another matter are Porter Nelson and D. R. C. Brown. They ask the County to give $1,000 for improvements to the Fair Grounds before the fair scheduled to be held in early October. Promoters say the fair will be the largest ever staged on the Western Slope, and will put Aspen at the top of the heap again. Nelson is working to get local merchants to advertise in the fair brochure, and also to promote the fair in Western Slope cities away from Aspen.

August 27, 1908 Mrs. S. I. Hallett gives a musical "in her elegant home" for her house guests. Reported among the invitees to the musical: D. R. C. Brown and Porter Nelson.

August 29, 1908 Clifford Miller again writes to urge Porter Nelson to move to Richmond. "Richmond weathered the financial storm with very few failures; in fact, I do not think the number was greater than in ordinary times and there were no failures for any large amount. The banks did not have to resort to the clearing house certificates and at all times let their customers have what money they needed."

September 2-3, 1908 The Colorado Telephone Company begins building a direct telephone line through Pearl Pass to connect Aspen in Pitkin County with Crested Butte in Gunnison County. The Pitkin County Democratic Convention picks 12 delegates to the State Democratic Convention in Pueblo, but Nelson is not one. The Democrat reports that Mrs. Porter Nelson and children will return to Colorado soon from Virginia to take up residence in Boulder for the winter.

September 15, 1908 The Democrat reports Porter Nelson's departure for Denver to meet his family who have been visiting in Culpeper, Virginia. Son Carmer enrolls at the University of Colorado in Boulder as a civil engineering student. Daughter Kate enters the College of Liberal Arts there, and joins the Kappa Kappa Gamma sorority.

October 2, 1908 The Peoples National Bank in Aspen gives notice that it is closing, and invites creditors to submit their claims for payment. Does Aspen need two banks?

October 8, 1908 Marble and Crystal Day at the Roaring Fork and Crystal River Fair in Aspen. Special excursion trains run from those towns. Redstone's benevolent capitalist Osgood sends Redstone residents and the town band to the Fair.

October 17, 1908 Mrs. S. I. Hallett invites the ladies who were in charge of the various events at the October 6-9 fair to tea to discuss improvements. The ladies decide to organize a Halloween masquerade ball to raise funds for the next fair.

October 22, 1908 B. Clark Wheeler buys control of the Aspen Times, presumably trying to enhance his bid for a seat in the Colorado Senate in the November 3, 1908 election. The Democrat reports rumors are floating that the Argentium-Juniata mine may start up again. As Secretary of the North Pole Mining Company, Porter Nelson begins publishing a new series of notices of a special meeting of the North Pole Mining Company, to be held at the Wheeler Opera House, November 2, 1908, to consider reorganization.

October 29, 1908 Deputy County Clerk Moses Bradshaw refuses to put the annexation question on the Pitkin County ballot on November 3. He says that it is not for the people of Pitkin County to vote on the proposed annexation of the Marble-Crystal area of Gunnison County. The ladies behind the Aspen Fair hold their masquerade ball at the Hotel Jerome. The price to dance: 75 cents per person, but single ladies and spectators can get in for only 25 cents.

November 1, 1908 The Democrat reports that Mrs. Porter Nelson and her daughter Marguerite are coming from Boulder to spend a few days with Mr. Nelson. She wants to cast her vote in the coming election in Aspen. Mr. and Mrs. D. R. C. Brown come to Aspen from Denver, for the same purpose.

November 3, 1908 Election Day. A special wire is set up at Aspen's Hotel Jerome so that interested persons can follow the latest results. To the disappointment of many in Aspen, Republican Taft defeats Democrat Bryan. Republicans continue to control the House and the Senate, but with reduced majorities. Despite Bryan's loss, the Democrat's choice of Denver for their convention pays off when Colorado votes

Democratic again. As usual, Pitkin County is solidly for the Democrats, with former Mayor Dr. Twining handily beating B. Clark Wheeler for a seat in state Senate. The Democrat headlines its report on the election: "Aspen People Gloomy Last Night - Taft Landslide Throughout the Country Made Us Weep. In Pitkin County, American Citizenship Prevails and Democracy is Supreme." The paper also praises the Chairman of the Pitkin Republicans, George Rohrbough, for graciously conceding the local Democratic victory. Mrs. W. Porter Nelson departs Aspen, along with the D. R. C. Browns and others who came for the election. Silver falls below 50 cents.

November 13, 1908 The Democrat reports that, despite the low price of silver, David Hyman has decided to go ahead with extensive development at his Smuggler mine. The Smuggler company renews for another five years its lease of the Della S. property. The Smuggler's "tin band" gives a concert at Redmen Hall, and the "Fair ladies" hold their regular weekly afternoon tea at the Hotel Jerome.

November 19, 1908 The Democrat reports that W. Porter Nelson and James Stewart are inspecting the Conundrum Gulch marble quarry for outside investors. If marble operations resume, a rail line will be built to the site from the Newman spur. The Yule Marble Company across the Elk Mountains is doing well with its white marble; why should not Conundrum Gulch also do well, with its dark marble?

November 25, 1908 The Democrat reports that Porter Nelson is going to Boulder to spend Thanksgiving with his family.

December 14, 1908 A French journal reveals that Senator Teller of Colorado told British bi-metallist Moreton Frewen that the US National Currency Commission is considering a plan to revive silver coinage, if the Indian Government agrees. Other members of the Commission, headed by Senator Nelson A. Aldrich, deny that the Commission is considering any such plan (the work of the Commission actually leads, in a few years, to the creation of the Federal Reserve System).

December 17, 1908 The direct telephone line between Aspen and Crested Butte in Gunnison County begins operation.

December 19, 1908 President Theodore Roosevelt returns to the Senate, unsigned, a Senate resolution changing, in Colorado's favor, the boundary of New Mexico Territory. The main sponsor of the resolution, Senator Henry Teller, says that the changes proposed were minor, involving only five postoffices. The Democrat reports that Porter Nelson will spend Christmas in Boulder with his family.

December 22, 1908 The Democrat praises the public spiritedness of John C. Osgood of Redstone on the completion of his "magnificent boulevard" from Carbondale to Redstone. About 18 miles of the new road are in Pitkin County, for which the County gave Osgood some financial help.

December 23, 1908 British bi-metallist Moreton Frewen claims that if the US and Britain increase purchases of silver, driving up the price of silver, Asian markets will have more buying power and will import more. He says that the resulting increase in US exports would pay for the Panama Canal.

December 24, 1908 Christmas being at hand, the rush tapers off at the mints for gold pieces. At its peak, demand was particularly heavy for \$2.50 and \$5 gold pieces. To meet demand, the mints turned out \$2 million in coins per day.

January 1, 1909 The silver price is now 50 1/4 cents an ounce, lead is \$4.15 a hundredweight. The Democrat reports that the San Francisco Mint has just completed one of the largest gold shipments ever made in the US. The California mint sent \$225.5 million in gold to the Denver mint, because (so the rumor went) Japan might attack the West Coast. At the start of the New Year, the Democrat reviews the Old Year. The mining outlook in Aspen at the start of 1908 was dim, with the best mines all inactive due to the low price of silver. A few lessees were at work in the Durant, A. J., Bushwhacker and the Millionaire properties. A few men stayed on at the Smuggler to keep pumps working and the mine thus in condition to be started up again. When on April 1, 1908 the Smuggler management said the Smuggler and Durant mines would reopen if miners would accept a wage of \$2.50, several hundred asked to work. Those hired stayed busy the rest of the year. In 1908, Colorado produced \$22.3 million in gold, an increase of \$2 million. Silver output fell to \$5.6 million due to the sharp silver price drop just before the year began.

January 20, 1909 Representative J. N. Ashby introduces a bill in the Colorado legislature calling for building a fish hatchery at Hallam Lake in Aspen. At last, some new development may be underway in Aspen.

January 27, 1909 In New York, the Mercantile Trust Company redeems the last silver bullion certificate of 1890.

Such certificates typically show that the issuing bank holds 1,000 ounces of silver bullion in its vaults. The certificates traded actively on the New York Stock Exchange during the 1890's when W. J. Bryan was a credible candidate pressing for silver remonetization. When banks first issued such certificates, silver cost about 60 cents an ounce; the Mercantile Trust paid 52.7 cents an ounce to pick up the last certificate.

January 30, 1909 The Democrat says that Porter Nelson is visiting relatives in Culpeper, Virginia. Left unsaid: he went East to explore further the idea of returning to Virginia.

February 12, 1909 A Julia Henry letter sent from Boulder to Porter in Culpeper shows Nelson finances under strain: "I have withdrawn $25 from my Denver account to pay the rent but will have to let the Daniels bill run a bit longer." She goes on: "I have stopped the Denver Post & had arranged to give up the piano but agreed to keep it until March 12 for $2." For her to give up her beloved piano is a real sacrifice. She lists certain expenditures she has made: rent-$30; gas-$6.15; telephone-$2.87; Dr. Williams-$22.00; Carmer's books-$5; Kate's books-$1.80; Marguerite's lab fee-$1.00.

February 17, 1909 Aspen Mayor Charles Wagner finds he has a good lease on the Mineral Farm property. He expects to ship out ore when he has his drift cleared.

February 20, 1909 Arriving in Denver to address a joint session of the legislature, W. J. Bryan says that he would consider making a fourth run for the Presidency if asked. He refuses to be drawn out on domestic affairs like silver, but attacks the Republicans over the Panama Canal.

March 1, 1909 The Aspen City Council approves a 1909 budget of $19,631, up from $17,316 in 1908.

March 10, 1909 From Boulder, Julia Henry again writes to Porter in Virginia: "You did not say on what basis you were to be assured of $2500 in Colorado. If it is the North Pole, I should be afraid to trust them. They would probably pay you two or three months and then shut down as they have done before. I think Clifford's offer is too good and generous to be turned down without a trial & I hope you will take it up for it might not be open indefinitely. I know you like Colorado and so do we all, but it would certainly seem to me we ought to do what is most sensible and safest . . . I hope you understand about Clifford's offer. I don't want you to do what you don't like but think that it is the safest thing and gives you the best future. Only we must be perfectly independent."

March 12, 1909 Julia Henry sends yet another letter to Porter about his brother-in-law Clifford Miller's offer of help in relocating: "I hope you will be able to make satisfactory arrangements with Clifford for it seems to me the best thing for you and the one that gives you the most future."

March 19, 1909 Julia Henry yet again urges her husband to relocate to Virginia: "I don't exactly understand the question you are waiting for us to decide. It seems to me an excellent proposition and far ahead of anything we could hope for in Colorado. We all like Colorado but feel we should go where we can do best. . . . I like Boulder better all the time but it does not seem much of a business place and we can't live on air and scenery. You must not say that your life is ruined.

You are too young and strong a man to feel that way, and when you are interested in a good strong business, everything will look entirely different to you. I am afraid it would be very difficult to find a position in Denver that would pay $2,000 and the trouble is we have nothing to live on in the meantime. The children feel the same way and are going to write you (Kate and Marguerite do so) but it is to be your business, so you are the one to decide the question after all."

March 20, 1909 The Democrat reports that the Colorado Attorney General is ready to sue Gifford Pinchot, the head of the US Forest Service, to compel the Government to open to claims under the Homestead Act five million acres of the Ute Indian Reservation in Colorado. He argues that this is required under the June 15, 1880 treaty by which the US took over the Indian lands. An early sagebrush revolt?

March 21, 1909 From Boulder, Kate writes to her father in Virginia: "I think Clifford's offer is dandy and you ought to accept it. I think that it is better than you could do in Denver. You can live on less in the East than you can in the West, at least you don't have to work so hard. You can hire someone to cook and do all the dishes for about half what you have to pay here. We couldn't expect Mother to work another year like she has had to work this. You say Carmer and I would have to give up college if we moved East. I don't see how we can go any better if you come West unless Mother works like a dog. Carmer won't come to Boulder another year anyway. If you don't take up the offer in the East, I don't see what will become of us. Please take it up for my sake. Try it for a year and then I am sure you will like it." Julia Henry writes too, saying "I think you would be making one of the greatest mistakes of your life if you don't accept it (Clifford Miller's proposal)." But Porter seems to think quitting Colorado would be an admission of failure.

March 27, 1909 A rumor is circulating in Aspen that the owners of the Mollie Gibson will repair the mill, and then reopen the mine and mill. It's just a rumor.

March 28, 1909 The Democrat reports that Carmer Nelson, after spending a week at the Dunlap Ranch on Capitol Creek, and a day in Aspen with friends, is returning to Boulder.

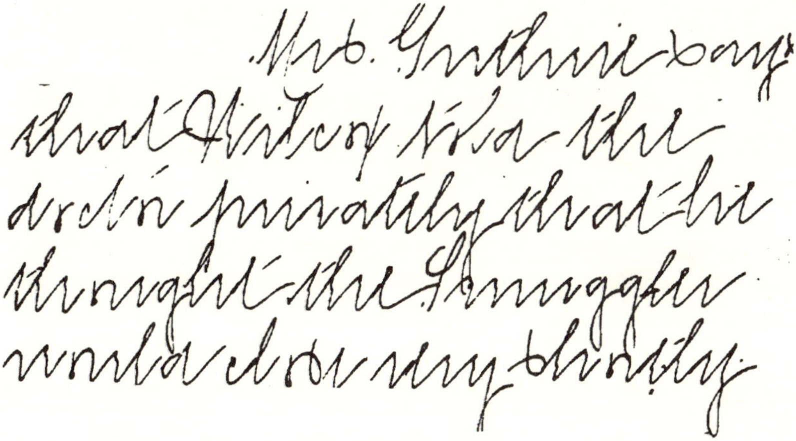

Above: Julia's distinctive penmanship, from a March 21, 1909 letter to her husband in Virginia. Translation: "Mrs. Guthrie said that Wilcox told the doctor privately that he thought the Smuggler would close very shortly."

April 3, 1909 The Democrat's lead article calls for Aspen business men to organize a Home Mining Company patterned after the successful Leadville model. The article asserts that there are good gold mining prospects south of Conundrum. "We made our money here, so let's spend it here!"

April 6, 1909 Democratic candidates sweep all the seats at stake in the Aspen municipal election.

April 13, 1909 The Democrat quotes new state Senator Twining as saying the Colorado Legislature has appropriated money to build a bridge over Maroon Creek, and to construct a fish hatchery along the Roaring Fork River. The paper says that Hallam Lake would be a good site for the hatchery, and that the City, County, and the Roaring Fork and Crystal River Fair Association would willingly make land available.

April 18, 1909 A certificate of incorporation is filed in Pitkin County for the Treasure Mountain Railroad Company. The Company plans to build a railroad up the Crystal River from Redstone in Pitkin County. This route would serve Marble and then cross over Anthracite Pass to Anthracite in Gunnison County. The backers of the railroad, who control the Crystal River Marble Company and the Tewks Mining Company, think the marble and slate beds found at the Yule Quarry extend across the river onto their land. Such a rail line would allow stone and ore from the Marble-Crystal area to reach the Rio Grande railhead at Anthracite. The Democrat laments that this line means the end of Pitkin County hopes of annexing the district. It says that Pitkin could have had the district for a song last November, but the machinations of some politicians prevented the people from voting on annexation. The Democrat headlines "Sidetrack your Calamity Lamentations, and Boost Aspen and Pitkin County on Their Merits. The District has a Future that Will Eclipse the Glorious Past." Two days later, the paper has this headline: "City of Aspen a Tourist Resort. Colorado Midland Places Advantages Before the People. It is Now Up to the People to Push It Along--Get in the Booster Wagon!"

May 4, 1909 Is the millionaire coming back to Aspen to live, with his new wife? A load of furniture arrives from Denver for D. R. C. Brown's new residence on Lake Avenue, and is put into storage while the house is repainted.

May 11,1909 Aspen and Pitkin County appropriate money to pay off the creditors of the Roaring Fork and Crystal River Fair Association. The City and County create a public authority to manage the old fair grounds and Hallam Lake. County Commissioner Fred Stockman is the authority's president, and Mayor Wagner is secretary. As Secretary of the North Pole Mining Company, Porter Nelson publishes a new notice of a special stockholders meeting to be held in the Wheeler Opera House building on June 14. The purpose of the meeting is to decide, again, on sale or reorganization of the company. The North Pole property is located near the top of Treasury Mountain, about half way from Marble to Crested Butte, with only poor transportation links to the outside world. But let's give them "A" for trying.

May 16, 1909 The new managers of the Hotel Jerome publish in the Democrat a notice to Aspen businessmen: "Some years ago, through your Commercial Club, you invested about $1,500 in improving the hotel. Now isn't it in your individual interest for all of you to boost this institution? Tell every drummer that you have a financial interest in your hotel and would appreciate their patronizing it."

<u>May 20, 1909</u> B. Clark Wheeler reportedly will reopen the Little Annie mine and mill. There are rumors of a rich silver-lead find at the Smuggler-Della S. mining complex.

<u>June 1, 1909</u> Porter Nelson borrows $2,000 from his widowed mother, Mary Elizabeth Nelson, at 6% interest. Other siblings borrow money from Mary Elizabeth, all at 6% interest. For example, his younger brother, Lewis, takes out four loans totaling over $10,000 between 1909 and 1915. These loans have no due date, and will be paid off by the borrowers from their shares in their mother's estate on her death. Sure, the loans give their mother steady income, but Porter certainly can use his share now in Colorado.

<u>June 3, 1909</u> The Yule company, operating the quarry at Marble, is planning to build substantial residences there. Famous mining engineer John Hays Hammond tells the Denver Chamber of Commerce that bi-metallism must be restored. The message is a welcome surprise, Hammond being a Republican.

<u>June 6, 1909</u> Having lost the election for a seat in the Colorado Senate, B. Clark Wheeler sells the <u>Aspen Times</u>. Aspen becomes a one newspaper town, with the <u>Democrat</u> taking over the <u>Times</u>. The first issue of the resulting paper appears under the name <u>Democrat-Times</u>.

<u>June 10, 1909</u> The silver price is 52 5/8 cents an ounce, lead $4.35 a hundredweight. The <u>Democrat-Times</u> reports that

Carmer Nelson is visiting in Aspen from the University at Boulder. The paper says that he will stay in town a few days before setting out for the Shuttleworth Ranch on Sopris Creek for the summer. In fact, Carmer will hold various summer jobs near Hotchkiss, where his family owns farm property.

June 18, 1909 Aspen is excited about reports of a gold strike up the Roaring Fork River from town. Ed Ogden and Frank Croman are the lucky discoverers. In Denver, the US Monetary League plans a petition drive to block a reported move in Congress to stop the circulation of silver dollars.

July 14, 1909 From Hotchkiss, Carmer Nelson writes to his father about his inspection of "our ranch." He reports that most of the peach trees there look healthy.

July 23, 1909 For himself, Carmer, Kate and Marguerite, Porter Nelson sells land in Culpeper County, Va. (deed book 43, page 124). This sale involves property received in 1906 from the estate of Lewis Porter Nelson.

August 28, 1909 Carmer Nelson, spending his vacation from the University of Colorado working on farms near Hotchkiss, writes his father about problems of growing peaches there.

October 1, 1909 A number of countries now are taking gold from the US. A Japanese purchase of $18 million of US gold prompts the National City Bank of New York to argue in its monthly newsletter that the Treasury should have some means of protecting the US gold supply from "arbitrary, unjustified" moves by foreign countries.

October 4, 1909 Four men from Denver, led by W. E. Bates, incorporate the Grand View Mesa Land and Orchard Company to take over farm land in Delta County, Colorado on Grand View Mesa (later known as Fruitland Mesa). Eighteen days later, three men, including the same W. E. Bates, incorporate the Grand View Reservoir and Canal Company in Delta County to purchase and operate the properties of the Grand View Canal and Irrigation Company, including the Aspen Ditch, the Castle Reservoir and other water systems. These Bates projects ultimately encompass the land and irrigation systems that Julia Henry bought in 1904, but only after difficult negotiations. At one point, Carmer writes his father fearing the deal with Bates will fall through.

February, 1910 Half way through his second year, Carmer Nelson gives up his engineering studies at Boulder. He instead takes up agriculture at Iowa State University in Ames.

April, 1910 The 13th Decennial Census places the population of Pitkin County at 4,566, down 2,100 from 1900. Aspen has lost proportionally more than the County. There is worse to come: Pitkin's population will fall to 2,707 in the 1920 census, and to 1,770 in the 1930 census before rising slightly to 1,836 in the 1940 census. The 1930 figure is less than 1/4 of that in the boom year of 1890. Few of Aspen's familiar names show up in the 1910 census. Samuel I. Hallett and wife are the exceptions. They are recorded as still living on West Francis Street, now without nieces or nephew with them. The 1910 census taker finds the Porter Nelson family at 1268 12th Street in Boulder; Nelson's occupation is given as real estate dealer (Roll 113, page 79, lines 29-33).

The Colorado Apple Is King

DELTA COUNTY challenges the world for fine fruit. THE GRAND VIEW MESA LAND AND ORCHARD COMPANY'S properties consist of some three thousand acres of the finest lands in the State of Colorado.

Situated in Delta County, in the heart of its most profitable peach and apple orchards, which are yielding the largest returns per acre of the best quality of fruit to be raised anywhere.

THESE ORCHARDS ARE PRODUCING

from three hundred to eight hundred dollars per acre of fruit each year.

THE GRAND VIEW MESA LAND AND ORCHARD COMPANY.

Do You Know

THESE BUSINESS MEN?

E. B. FIELD...President, The Colorado Telephone Co.
F. G. MOFFAT.... ...Cashier, First National Bank.
JAMES A. McCLURG ....Mining Engineer
A. D. LEWIS...President, A. D. Lewis Dry Goods Co.
J. C. GALLUP. ...Real Estate and Investments.
Wm. V. HODGES ....Attorney at Law.
R. A. SAVAGEAU .... Merchandise Broker.
C. W. KEITH.. .....Farm Implements and Vehicles.
PHILLIP ARGALL ....Mining Engineer.
W. F. R. MILLS..Late Sec. Denver Chamber Commerce.
W. F. WEBB...President The Program Publishing Co.
W. F. WOLFF...... .... .Real Estate.
E. L. OGDEN..President, The Ogden Dry Goods Co.
GEO. R. PARK...... ... ...Stockman.
W. PORTER NELSON... .. ....Mining.
G. O. ARGALL.... ....Mining.
W. E. Bates... ... Real Estate and Investments.

Stockholders or Directors and Officers of

The Grand View Mesa Land & Orchard Company

<u>Advertisement of orchard land near Hotchkiss, CO. after Nelson joins forces with Bates</u>

November 8, 1910 In the off year elections, the Republicans lose seats in the Senate, but retain control. Democrats take control of the House, but the party is no longer Bryan's tool.

Porter Nelson is gone for good from Aspen, but he still has mining interests on the Western slope. The Democrats now support gold mono-metallism, although a few diehards still hope for government support for silver. We can't end the Nelson-silver story just yet.

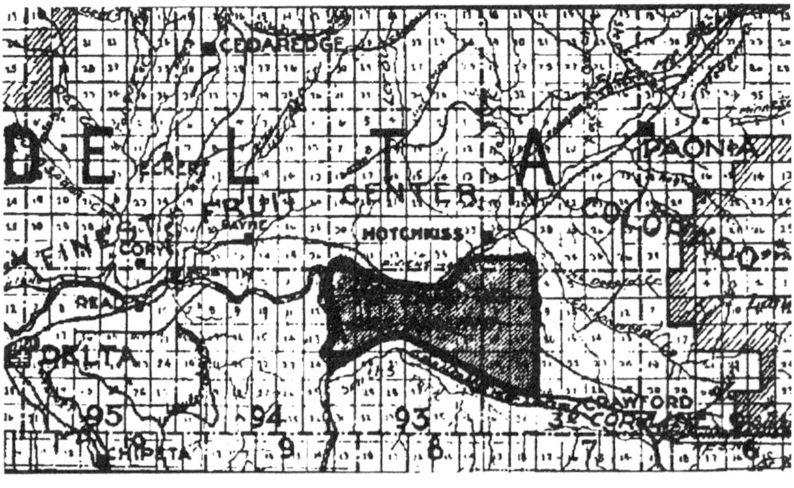

Map of Grand View Mesa lands

CHAPTER TEN

LIFE AFTER ASPEN

Early 1911 The 1911 Denver City Directory shows Porter Nelson as Treasurer, Treasury Mountain Metals Company. Treasury Mountain is in the Crystal mining district.

January 23, 1911 J. Henry Nelson buys at a tax sale a 20/96 th interest in the Robert E. Lee lode mining claim in the Tin Cup mining district of Gunnison County. Porter had bought an interest in this claim in 1891, and Julia Henry had bought a 15/24 th share in 1901. Both Julia Henry and Porter being from the old Confederacy, they must like the name Robert E. Lee. The Tin Cup district is a gold area near Taylor Park. Origin of the name: a cowboy using an old cup to get a drink of water from a stream found flakes of gold in the cup. There is now a water reservoir in Taylor Park.

March 27, 1911 Carmer Nelson writes his father from Ames: "So Dr. Twining has bought the house. Well, I would rather think of it occupied than going to rack and ruin empty. I feel sure that if you do want to get a house in Aspen this summer, you can obtain one for almost nothing." The house Twining is buying lies on lots C, D and E of Block 29 in Aspen. The 1910 tax list shows this property as Nelson's, and that Nelson's immediate neighbors there are Harold Clark on one side, and Alonzo Frye on the other. Block 29 lies between 4th and 5th Streets, and Bleeker and Hallam Streets.

June 19, 1911 In Denver, Porter Nelson executes a note for $2,500 in favor of N. H. Griffith, secured by a 1/3 interest in the N. H. Griffith Company. The note bears 6% interest. Nelson in effect is borrowing money from Griffith to buy a share in Griffith's firm. Nelson could have borrowed money from Clifford Miller to buy into a company in Richmond.

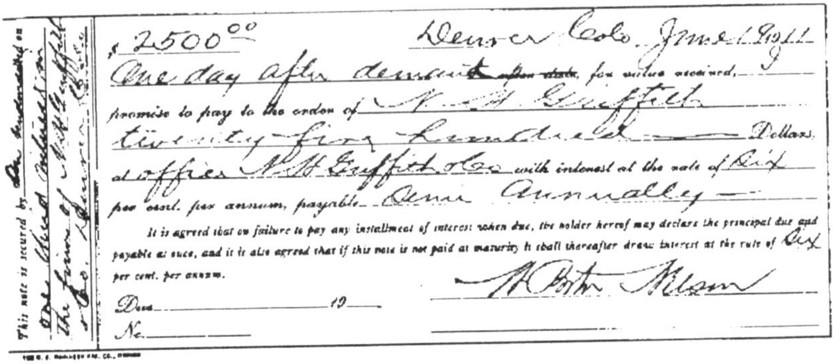

$2500.00 Denver Colo. June 1 1911

One day after demand for value received, I promise to pay to the order of N. H. Griffith

twenty-five hundred Dollars

at office N. H. Griffith & Co. with interest at the rate of six per cent. per annum, payable Semi Annually

It is agreed that on failure to pay any installment of interest when due, the holder hereof may declare the principal due and payable at once, and it is also agreed that if this note is not paid at maturity it shall thereafter draw interest at the rate of six per cent. per annum.

H. Porter Nelson

Due ______ 19__

No. ______

This note is secured by one hundred shares in the firm of N. H. Griffith & Co. Denver Colo.

Nelson's IOU to Griffith

July 25, 1911 As company secretary, Porter Nelson files at the Pitkin County Courthouse, the certificate of incorporation of the Colorado Highland Marble Company. Stated capital is $1 million. The company plans to take over and operate the old dark marble quarry in Conundrum Gulch.

November 17, 1911 The Mint reports that in 1910, the US produced $96 million of gold, and $57 million of silver. Gold output was $3 million less than in 1909, due to falling output in Alaska, but silver output increased $1.3 million.

January 1, 1912 Early estimates place US gold production in 1911 at $96 million, unchanged from 1910. Silver production at 57.8 million ounces was down slightly from 1910, with all but 24 million going to the Treasury. In 1911, the Mint turned out $56 million in gold coins, and $5.6 million in silver coins. The Denver City Directory for 1912 shows that Porter Nelson is Manager of the Insurance Department of the N. H. Griffith Company. He still has a 1/3 ownership share.

<u>January 25, 1912</u> A letter to the Editor of the <u>New York Times</u> says that the Treasury is holding 479 million silver dollars as backing for $455 million in silver certificates. As bullion, each of those silver dollars is worth only 40 cents. The letter writer asks: should not the Treasury suspend further purchases of silver bullion, and meet its needs by melting down the silver dollars on hand? The Treasury's existing supply of dollars will last for many years.

<u>June, 1912</u> With the class of 1912, Kate Nelson graduates from the University of Colorado.

Kate Nelson .... Boulder

ΚΚΓ

President Woman's League (4); Mortar Board (4); Y. W. C. A. Cabinet (4); Associate Editor "Coloradoan" (3); Vice-Pres. Y. W. C. A. (2) (3); Girls' Tennis Club (4); Manager Y. W. C. A. Circus (3).

"When unadorned, adorned the most."

Kate Nelson in the 1913 <u>Coloradoan</u>

<u>Political Conventions, 1912</u> The Republicans convene again in Chicago, nominate Taft. Their platform endorses the gold standard and a new currency system, a harbinger of the Federal Reserve System. The Bull Moose faction splits away

to name ex-President Theodore Roosevelt as its candidate for President. Their platform attacks the so-called Aldrich bill "because it would place our currency and credit system in private hands, not subject to effective public control." Despite Bull Moose opposition, the Aldrich Bill passes the next year, with some modifications. The Democrats convene in Baltimore and name Woodrow Wilson of New Jersey as their candidate. Wilson is no supporter of silver. Their platform also hints at the establishment of a new currency system, under which "our country will be largely freed from panics and consequent unemployment and business depressions by such a systematic revision of our banking laws as will render temporary relief in localities where such relief is needed." The Democrats oppose the Aldrich Bill, and the establishment of a central bank. Times change: in 1913, a Democratic Congress and President will approve creating the Federal Reserve System.

<u>October 6, 1912</u> More currency is in circulation in the United States than ever before, $3.306 billion. Gold coin and gold certificates make up almost half this amount, and bank notes account for another $750 million. The rising price of silver in the US reflects speculation on the possible need of China, a silver country, to obtain silver to pay its soldiers after the Revolution of 1911. Also speculation on the need of India, another silver country, to increase its silver coinage.

<u>November 5, 1912</u> Profiting from Republican bickering, Wilson wins the White House, the first Democrat to do so in 30 years. The Democrats capture both the House and Senate, ending 30 years of Republican control of the latter body. But no help for silver; the Democrats are no longer pushing to restore the glory of the white metal.

January 21, 1913 In Aspen, shareholders of the Meadow Mountain Mining Company (MMM) approve reorganization of the company. They also approve issuance of new notes of indebtedness bearing interest at 12% per annum in exchange for outstanding notes. Porter Nelson is Assistant Secretary-Treasurer of this company, which owns mines in Crystal.

March 7, 1913 For himself and as trustee for his children Carmer, Kate and Marguerite, Porter Nelson, sells land in Culpeper County, Va. (deed book 49, pages 253 and 255). The parcel is a tract of 29 acres near Rixeyville that had been part of his father's estate. The stated price: $10. The notary fee on the deed is $1. No big money here.

June 5, 1913 Carmer Nelson graduates from the Colorado Agricultural College at Fort Collins. The next year, Marguerite, Porter and Julia Henry's third child, graduates from the University of Colorado at Boulder. A pretty good education record for a family whose finances have been rocky.

1914-16 Denver city directories for this period show Porter Nelson still at the N. H. Griffith Company, and manager of the insurance department. The Griffith Company apparently is not a solid operation. In a 1915 letter to his father, Carmer Nelson commiserates about the depression gripping Denver, and refers to the shaky condition of the Griffith Company. The average price for silver bullion in London in 1915 is a record low, 23 3/4 pence an ounce, equivalent to 48.3 US cents. Silver will rise from there (but will set an even lower record price in the Depression). In 1916, Nelson persuades his mother to lend the Griffith Company $1,000 at 7% interest, 1% more than he agreed to pay Griffith. He personally guarantees that the loan will be repaid. This money enables the Griffith Company to buy up Porter Nelson's share.

1917 US entry into World War I increases the demand for metals and boosts mineral production of all kinds. The wartime boost would be only temporary, but it gives Porter Nelson the opportunity to work again for himself. The 1917 Denver City Directory shows him working on his own in the Kittredge Building. He will stay there until WW II, when he is forced to move to the California Building.

February 18, 1917 Mary Elizabeth Nelson, Porter Nelson's mother, dies in Richmond, Virginia. Porter's debt to her is extinguished, and he comes into more inherited money.

March 9, 1918 Porter Nelson sells to L. U. Guggenheim of Denver a 2/3 rd interest in the Lucky Boy mining claim on Sheep Mountain near Crystal.

April 9, 1918 Senator Key Pittman of Nevada, supported by Treasury Secretary McAdoo, introduces a "war emergency" bill. The bill calls for melting all silver dollars lying unused in the Treasury, and for replacing silver certificates with other types of currency. While the mint has coined no silver dollars since 1904, much silver is tied up in the hundreds of millions of unwanted silver dollars just gathering dust in the Treasury. Silver is needed for subsidiary coinage, and the US would like to use silver bullion, not gold, to settle unfavorable trade balances with many countries, especially those in the silver loving Orient. As a gesture towards silver miners, the bill also raises the Treasury buying price for silver from 91 cents an ounce to $1.00, subject to the prevailing seignorage fee.

April 23, 1918 The Pittman Silver Coinage Act (40 Stat. 535) becomes law just two weeks after its introduction. No Capitol Hill gridlock then. Collectors in later years bemoan this melting down of silver dollars.

May 7, 1918 The Viceroy of India thanks the United States for its action making more silver available to India.

July 15, 1918 Eight men from Denver file 22 placer mine location claims to oil shale in the Petrolite Mining District of Rio Blanco County (book 53, pages 262 to 273). The claims are known as Sid numbers 1-22. Porter Nelson later buys these claims, probably during the Great Depression when unpatented oil shale claims trade for a few cents per acre.

December 1, 1919 Porter Nelson buys for himself, through E. L. Ogden as trustee, all the property of the Inez Mining Company, in which he had been a large shareholder. This includes Inez lode claims nos. 1-13, and the Gray Copper and Pointer lodes near Crystal. This purchase is recorded in Gunnison records only on October 15, 1934. Like Nelson, Ogden is gone from Aspen; in 1934, he is in Longmont.

February 2, 1920 In Denver, Julia Henry executes a new deed of sale for the Jessie G. and Fresno lodes in the Cripple Creek mining district. For some reason her first deed of sale, recorded December 17, 1900, was found defective. The Nelsons now have sold all their onetime holdings in the Cripple Creek gold area.

February 25, 1920 The Mineral Lands Leasing Act (41 Stat 437) comes into force, ended further patenting of location claims for oil shale, also for other fuel and fertilizer minerals. Extracting such materials from federal land henceforth will be subject to lease and royalty payments. But the law does not wipe out valid claims pending on this date, including the Sid claims no. 1-22. Disputes about grandfathered claims will continue for years. Hard rock mineral mining is not affected by the Act and continues free of lease and royalty payments.

May, 1920 Porter Nelson advises shareholders of Meadow Mountain Mining Company of an offer from the large Gold Reserve Mining Company of Chicago to take over the MMM Company in a one-for-one exchange of stock. The Chicago firm offers another 20,000 shares of Gold Reserve stock to be used to compensate holders of MMM notes. Nelson urges acceptance of the offer, but the deal does not go through.

1920's World production of silver is about 300 million ounces a year. China and India consume about 80% of that output. In 1922, US mints turn out 51,000,000 silver dollars, a figure that still stands as record yearly output.

December 21, 1921 Julia Henry Nelson dies in Denver. She had entered St. Joseph's Hospital a week earlier after breaking her hip in a fall. She was progressing well when a sudden onset of pneumonia caused her death in a just few hours. Her obituary in the Rocky Mountain News the next day described her as the wife of a widely known pioneer mining man.

August 3, 1922 Porter Nelson helps incorporate the Grand View Canal and Irrigation Company in Delta County, for 20 years. The Company is capitalized at $218,750. It will take over and operate the water systems of the similarly named company organized in 1909 for 20 years. Nelson holds 1/4 of the shares and is secretary of the new company. Promoter H. E. Bates seems to be out of it entirely.

March 14, 1923 In Hotchkiss, the new Grand View Mesa Irrigation Canal Company holds its first shareholders meeting.

January 26, 1926 Porter Nelson seeks to postpone a meeting of the shareholders of the Meadow Mountain Mining Company scheduled for this date in Aspen. The reason: an important adjudication of water rights is to be held in Hotchkiss, Colorado on efforts by the state of California to appropriate water from Colorado streams. Nelson must attend that.

1929-32 The Great Depression starting in October, 1929 makes conditions even worse for silver miners. By 1930, the silver price is down almost 40% from 1926. World silver production in 1932 falls to only 165 million ounces, vs. 260 million ounces in 1929. In Denver, Porter Nelson gives up his large house on East 12th street, having little money, no family and being away on business so much of the time.

June 29, 1930 Aspen's sole remaining millionaire, David R. C. Brown dies at his Aspen home. The New York Times considers Brown important and publishes an obituary on July 1, 1930, something it had not done when Brown's wealthy father-in-law, Henry Cowenhoven, died in 1896.

March 7-11, 1932 The House Committee on Coinage holds hearings on H. R. 72, proposing a study on the causes and effects of the then prevailing low price of silver. The House in the end takes no action on the bill.

November-December, 1932 Porter Nelson explains to the Aspen State Bank that since May, irrigators have not paid for the water drawn from the Grand View Irrigation Canal Company of which Nelson is Secretary. That bank holds a mortgage coming due November 18 on the company's Aspen Ditch. Silver falls to 24 1/4 cents an ounce on December 29, 1932, still the record low price of the white metal.

March, 1933 Current silver price: 27 1/2 cents an ounce. Left languishing as Franklin D. Roosevelt is inaugurated is the bill of Rep. Andrew Somers of New York, authorizing the Treasury to buy 40 million ounces of silver a month, at a price up to 75 cents an ounce. A New Yorker helping silver?

May 12, 1933 Congress passes the National Economic Emergency Act (48 Stat. 31), designed primarily to relieve distress on the farm. The last part of the Act (sometimes separately called the Coinage Parity Act) gives the President power to change the weight of the gold dollar and of the silver dollar. It also gives the President authority to receive foreign silver, valued at 50 cents on the dollar, in payment of foreign government debts to the US.

June-July, 1933 A 66-nation World Economic and Monetary Conference opens in London on June 12. A week later, the chief US delegate, Senator Pittman of Nevada, proposes that gold remain the prime standard of value, but that gold be withdrawn from circulation and placed in reserves. More currency should be issued against existing reserves until the reserve level falls to 25%. Thirty per cent of a country's reserves should be held in gold, and a further 20% in either silver or gold. Subsidiary silver coinage should be remonetized and not further debased. The chief silver producing countries should limit sales on the world market. On July 1, the conference adopts a declaration ad referendum that the gold standard should be restored, and governments and central banks should act to stem currency speculation. President Franklin Roosevelt refuses to agree to this declaration, annoying many other countries. Nonetheless, Pittman persuades eight countries most involved with silver to adopt a US proposal. The proposal calls on governments to eschew the practice of melting down or debasing silver currency, to replace low value paper currency with silver coins, and to adopt no legislation that would depreciate silver. Major silver users (China, India and Spain) and major silver producers (Australia, Canada, US, Mexico and Peru) reach a separate agreement to withhold silver from the world market between 1934 and 1937. Under it, China agrees not to release onto the market any silver derived from melting down or debasing silver coinage. India agrees to limit to less than 35 million ounces per year its sales of silver. Spain agrees to limit its disposal over those four years to no more than 5 million ounces of silver per year. The silver producing countries commit themselves to withholding 35 million ounces of silver from the market during the same years. The US agrees to withhold the most silver, committing itself to freeze over 24 million ounces a year. The Conference fails to set an agreed silver-to-gold price ratio, something the US has sought since 1878. Still the US does get, in much weakened form, one long sought objective: an international agreement on silver.

December 21, 1933 President Franklin D. Roosevelt issues a proclamation carrying out the agreement reached in London by silver users and silver producers (48 Stat. 1723). Roosevelt orders the mint to begin accepting newly mined, domestic silver bullion for unlimited coinage. Silverites had long sought "free" coinage, but the proclamation says that those bringing silver bullion to the Mint for coinage must give the Treasury as seignorage 1/2 of the silver presented. Still, with the market price for silver 47.5 cents an ounce, and the Treasury in effect paying 64 1/2 cents net, it's a good deal.

January 30-31, 1934 Congress passes the Gold Reserve Act of 1934 (48 Stat. 337). The Act reinforces the President's authority to cut the value of the dollar, now by up to 50%. Other sections of the Act provide for unlimited coinage of silver, ban circulation of gold coins in the US, and call for the Treasury to take over the gold holdings of the Federal Reserve. President Roosevelt promptly issues a Revaluation of Gold Proclamation (48 Stat. 1730) cutting the weight of the gold dollar by 41%. This raises the price of gold to $35 an ounce. Leaving the silver dollar unchanged, the proclamation makes the silver-to-gold ratio 27:1, far from the old 16:1.

June 19, 1934 Congress passes the Silver Purchase Act (48 Stat. 1178). The Act calls for the Treasury to buy silver from any source and hold it until silver makes up 1/4 of the total US monetary stock of gold and silver. The purchase price may not be in excess of the coinage value of silver ($1.29 an ounce). This Act certainly will bring in enough silver to meet the US stockpiling commitment made in London. For the next 30 years, the Treasury is the major force in the world silver market, buying when the price was low (as it usually was), and selling when the price was high (as happened later). At the peak in the late 1950's, the Treasury controls 3.5 billion ounces of silver, just 1/4 of that coming from US mines. By its purchases, the Treasury helps silver miners not just in the US, but all over the world.

<u>August 16, 1935</u> Senator Key Pittman prsuades the Senate to approve Resolution 187. This Resolution calls for the establishment of a Special Committee of five Senators to consider the operation of the Silver Purchase Act (48 Stat 1178). In 1935, mints at Philadelphia and San Francisco turn out the last 1.9 million of "regular" silver dollars. "Regular" silver dollars will circulate in Nevada casinos for years.

<u>June 28, 1936</u> Porter Nelson buys from H. H. Williams three lode mining claims in the Crystal area (Bon Ton, Gray Copper, and Lucky Boy), and three mill sites (Gray Copper, Mammoth and Cleopatra). Does he think these mines could become active again, or is the price just too low to pass up?

<u>December 31, 1938</u> President Roosevelt issues an Executive Order extending the silver purchase program for another 6 months. It otherwise would have expired on this day. US silver purchases have been holding the world market price of silver between 44 and 46 1/2 cents an ounce.

<u>March 21, 1939</u> Senator Pittman's Special Committee on Silver holds hearings on a bill to change the status of the Federal Reserve. The bill would make the Federal Reserve Board of Governors purely a government agency, the Monetary Authority. This Authority would be charged with regulating, adjusting and stabilizing the value of the dollar. The bill also envisages that Congress's Constitutional power to "regulate" money be interpreted as permitting the Authority to adjust the value of the dollar to serve the best interests of the people

and the domestic economy. The bill goes nowhere, but shows that questions exist about the role of the Federal Reserve Board in the light of Congress's power to "regulate" coinage.

Spring, 1939 Porter Nelson hopes to find a promoter to buy his land in Delta County, and retail it to farm-raised East Europeans. Many of these are now retiring, with nest eggs, from steel plants or coal mines and may want to farm again.

Nelson's 1939 draft advertisement for Farm Sale

I R R I G A T E D L A N D
Grand View Mesa, Delta County, Colorado
4 to 6 miles South of Hotchkiss

This land is a rich mesa soil, very fertile and has the necessary minerals to produce abundant crops. It is irrigated by the Grand View canal that furnishes sufficient water, during the irrigation season, to cover the land to the depth of three feet. With Colorado's almost constant sunshine, and moisture available to be applied when needed, this makes for big crops. Wheat produces from 35 to 50 bushels per acre, barley from 50 to 75 bushels and other crops proportionally. Alfalfa is the favorite hay crop; all fruits and berries do well. Apple and peach orchards have produced from $500 to $1250 per acre, but are special crops requiring expert care. This land once sold, during the fruit boom, at $200 per acre in 10 acre tracts. Later it was sold as farm lands for $75 to $100 an acre; during the depression it sold at $40 to $50 an acre, with occasional sales below these prices. The land is subdivided into 80, 120, and 160 acre tracts with farm improvements on each. The tracts are now rented to tenants for the year 1939 - subject to prior sale. The price is $30 an acre, 50% commission to him who buys and retails to clients.

Year end, 1941 Porter Nelson visits his remaining family members in Virginia. The question again arises: should he return to his roots, where many are still ready to help him?

April, 1942 The US Government leases the Kittredge Building in Denver, minus the ground floor. Porter Nelson must leave the premises he has occupied for 25 years. He asks the Bureau of Mines Office in Denver how the Government will pay the promised bonus to persons who deliver strategic mineral ore to smelters for refining. From Denver, Porter Nelson replies to a renewed invitation to return to Virginia extended by his well-off sister, Lucille Miller. He tells Lucille frankly what his assets are: five small, irrigated farms totalling 580 acres in Delta County, and some mining properties, mostly in the Crystal area. He says the farms carry mortgages of $7 an acre, and the mines are worthless unless someone one can be found to work them (presumably as lessees). He says that on his previous visit to Virginia, he had told his younger brother Lewis that he would try to sell his Colorado holdings and go to Culpeper to help Lewis manage property inherited from their father. Curiously, in describing his assets, Nelson does not mention any oil shale claims. After his death, his Sid oil shale claims no. 1-22 will turn out to be his most valuable holdings. In 1942, had he not yet bought these?

June 11, 1942 Charles F. Garlington of Carbondale, Porter Nelson's eyes and ears in Aspen, writes that the American Smelting and Refining Company has just exercised two options on mines in Pitkin County. Also, this company is sending someone in a few days to see Garlington about an option that Nelson holds from a Mrs. Wright in Denver to sell or lease the Park Regent mine near Aspen that she inherited from her husband's father. Can he yet make a profit in Aspen?

June 25, 1942 Porter Nelson files a certificate in Delta County making the Grand View Canal and Irrigation Company a perpetual corporation. The stated capital now is to $43,750, down from $218,750 twenty years earlier. This decrease confirms the rule: Nelson enterprises decline in value.

October 6, 1942 The War Production Board decides to end gold mining in the US, to free men and equipment for mining strategic, nonferrous metals. Silver, which has war time uses, is not affected by the shut down.

May 3, 1943 Congress passes the Suspension of Annual Assessment Work Act (57 Stat. 74) allowing holders of unpatented mining claims to file notice in the appropriate county instead of performing the required $100 worth of annual assessment work. The suspension will last until the first July 1 after the end of World War II hostilities (the end later is proclaimed to be December 31, 1946).

June 22, 1943 As permitted under the law of May 3, 1943, Porter Nelson files notice in the Rio Blanco County court house that he is suspending development work on the Sid nos. 1-22 oil shale claims. When he took over these claims is not easily determined from the records of Rio Blanco County.

July 12, 1943 With World War II imposing heavy demands on available silver, Congress passes the Silver Use Act (57 Stat. 520) permitting the Treasury to supply silver for war needs irrespective of the Silver Coinage Ratio Act of 1934. Wartime copper shortages induce the Treasury to lend out some of its stock of silver for use as a copper substitute.

May 11, 1944 Porter Nelson deeds to the Delta County Public Trustee certain property in that county on which he no longer wishes to pay taxes. The next year he sells to private parties certain other Delta County properties.

<u>June 28, 1944</u> Nelson writes his sister Lucille that he will be coming to Virginia on a visit soon after July 10. This visit will turn out to be Nelson's last to Virginia.

<u>October 7, 1944</u> Back in Denver, Nelson writes his sister Lucille that he recently advertised two Delta County farms for sale, and received 100 requests for information about them. He complains that it is hotter in Denver now than it was at any time in Culpeper during his July visit there.

<u>July 31, 1946</u> The Silver Industrial Use Act (60 Stat 750) comes into force. It provides that the Treasury may sell off for industrial use some of its huge hoard of silver, at a price not less than 90.3 cents an ounce, provided enough silver is retained to redeem all outstanding silver certificates. A sop to silver miners: the bill cuts the seignorage charge on domestic, newly mined silver presented to the Mint for coinage to 30%, down from the 45% set in 1939.

<u>December 24, 1946</u> Porter Nelson dies in Denver, age 84. His survivors are two children and eight grandchildren. A brief obituary, appearing on page 2 of the <u>Denver Post</u> of December 25, describes him as "a mining man" who came to Colorado in 1888 from Culpeper, Virginia and who for many years pursued mining interests from Aspen and Denver. This brief obituary really doesn't do justice to the long life of W. Porter Nelson.

My hope is to compensate for this shortcoming.

CHAPTER ELEVEN

DETOUR TO CRYSTAL

The reader will have noted that, after 1893, Aspen press and mining circles closely watched what was going on in the little town of Crystal, a few miles to the west, as the crow flies, across the Elk mountains. Porter Nelson was among the many attracted to Crystal. In 1890, he bought his first property in the Rock Creek mining district (the formal name for the Crystal mining area). He bought Crystal property as late as the 1930's while buying no more property in Pitkin County after the first years of the 20th century. During the World War I mining boom, he even undertook some limited mining operations in Crystal. When he died, he still owned many Crystal properties. I must say more about Crystal.

My mother, Kate Nelson Houston, died in 1932. To keep up family ties and wanting his Echternach and Houston grandchildren to get to know one another, my grandfather Nelson in the summer of 1936 proposed a joint vacation at his beloved cabin at Crystal. Coming from Kansas City, we Houstons picked Porter Nelson up in Denver and then drove to Glenwood Springs to meet the Echternachs. They were driving to Glenwood from Beverly Hills, California. After a get-acquainted swim in the Glenwood pool, we planned to be off the next morning for Crystal. The road wasn't paved, but we expected no problems, given the high clearance of cars of the time. Sadly, a mud slide on the road above Redstone blocked us. While waiting to see if the road might be cleared, my grandfather took me to see a small hydro-power plant at Redstone using a Pelton turbine. Pretty neat way to get electricity, I remember thinking. Sadly, the mud slide was not trivial; we settled for a cabin on the Grand Mesa for our vacation. I had to wait 51 more years to get to Crystal.

Crystal is quite well isolated from most of Gunnison County. The February 23, 1881 Act of the Colorado legislature establishing Pitkin County says the Pitkin boundary runs in a northwesterly or westerly direction along the summit of the Elk mountain range from the National Range (i. e. Continental Divide) to Snow Mass Mountain, and from there due West to the divide west of Rock Creek (Crystal River). Why did the legislature chose Snow Mass Mountain as the anchor, instead of some more southerly peak leaving the Crystal River drainage intact? Presumably because Crystal already existed in 1881 and its access then was solely from Gunnison County. Modern society compensates for the short-sightedness of the 1881 legislation. The telephone company lists Marble numbers with those in Pitkin, Garfield and Eagle counties, not with Gunnison. Since snow in winter blocks the high passes to the Marble-Crystal area from Gunnison County, that County arranges for emergency services from Eagle County (why did Gunnison not choose adjoining Pitkin?).

When my grandfather Nelson had little money of his own, he tried creative ways of making money in Crystal:

<u>July 12, 1922</u> Having in 1917 sold a 2/3 share in his dormant Lucky Boy mine to L. U. Guggenheim of Denver, Nelson now persuades the latter to join in creating a corporation, the Lucky Boy Mines Company. Nelson is Secretary-Treasurer. The Company will work three patented claims, and five unpatented claims held by location, all on Sheep Mountain near Crystal. The two owners take common stock for their interests and will try to sell 8% preferred shares to outside investors. If (big if) they can sell the preferred shares, they will reopen the mine. Nelson names his sons-in-law, A. V. Echternach, a Los Angeles advertising man,

and R. B. Houston, an Interstate Commerce Commission engineer, to the Board of Directors. Results? Apparently nothing substantial.

November 11, 1924 Engineers say that 150 million KWH of electricity could be produced each year from the 180,000 acre feet of water falling on the basins around Crystal. For "one dollar and other valuable considerations," Porter Nelson sells to George W. Ray of Chicago one-half the profits to be made in a Crystal River power project Nelson is promoting.

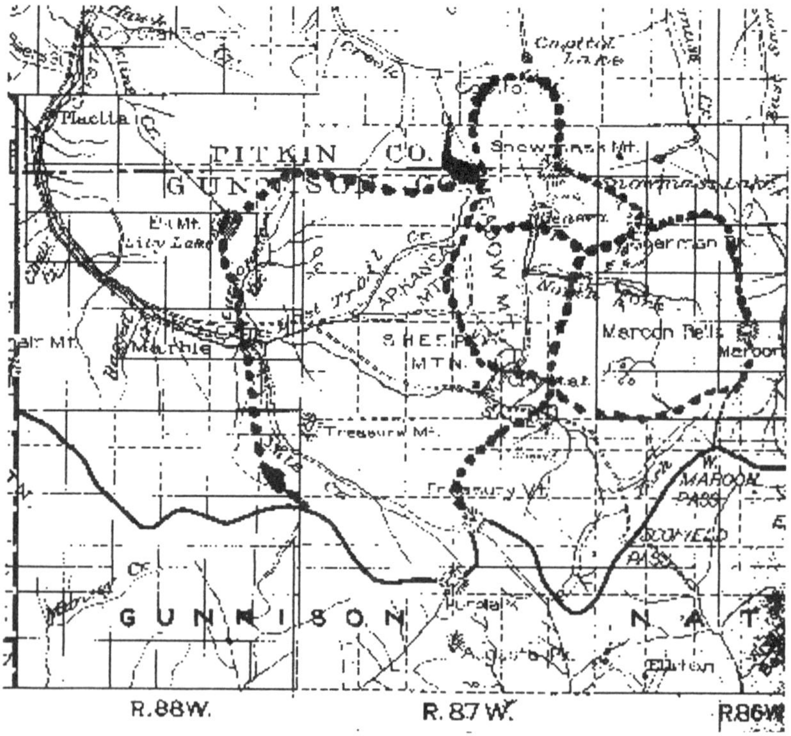

Catchment areas of Nelson's proposed Crystal River Power Projec

After the end of the first year, Ray may continue his interest in the project by paying what is required to keep the filings and title in good standing at the office of State Engineer who regulates power projects. At the end of the year, Nelson informs Ray that his rights are lapsing due to Ray's failure to keep up his payments. This power project is never built.

July, 1928 Nelson helps to organize the Treasury Mountain Mining Company to take over the North Pole, Shakespeare and other copper mining claims high up on Treasury Mountain near Crystal. Other organizers are Nathan Sturdy, an unrelated H. M. Nelson and P. W. Driver. Again, Nelson serves as company Secretary. The company is not a success.

March 28, 1940 Porter Nelson writes to a mining broker to describe various Crystal properties he owns, or on which he has the disposal rights. These are: 27 lode mining claims in the Black Queen group; the Lead King group, which includes the Meadow Mountain Mining properties; the Sheep Mountain group of about a dozen claims; the Inez Group of 15 claims; the Lucky Boy group of five properties; the Bon Ton group, consisting in part of lapsed claims; the Commonwealth Placer of 160 acres; the North Pole and Shakespeare Group of 18 patented claims and several unpatented claims; and also the Harris-Fairly Group of three patented claims. He also wants to sell the preliminary work he has done toward building an electric power plant on the Crystal River, and some lots in Crystal. He asks $60,000 for all, but no sale results.

April 6, 1944 Porter Nelson writes George Gaskell of the Colorado Zinc Co. in Alhambra, California that he is mailing executed leases on the Lost Horse and Lead King mines, as well as assignments of his 1/3 interest in the Lucky Boy mine, and a deed to a cabin and a lot in Crystal. Colorado Zinc is to pay Nelson $100 a month as a royalty advance.

<u>May 19, 1944</u> Gaskell, who wants to take over the Sheep Mountain property, writes Porter Nelson that the man to whom Nelson has optioned the Sheep Mountain group, Nathan Sturdy, lacks funds to operate those mines. Nelson replies proposing that Sturdy be given time to work things out.

<u>May 25, 1944</u> Nelson tells Gaskell that he is getting old and wishes to dispose of everything. Nelson suggests that Gaskell raise enough money to buy all his Crystal property.

<u>June 17, 1944</u> Porter Nelson responds to a renewed bid from Gaskell to buy the Sheep Mountain properties. Nelson asks that the matter rest until he can get clear title. He explains that his daughter, Kate Nelson Houston, held an interest in the property when she died, leaving an heir who is still a minor (Richard N. Houston, born in 1929). Under Colorado law, it is impossible to get clear title by a tax sale against an insane person or a minor. In the end, this deal with Gaskell does not go through.

<u>March 17, 1945</u> For years, George Harris in Marble had acted as Nelson's agent in the Crystal mining district. Nelson now writes to Harris asking about the status of certain mining claims on Crystal's Sheep Mountain. Nelson expresses the hope of getting into the field that summer. Even at age 83, after so many dashed hopes, Nelson remains interested in Crystal.

Was Porter Nelson justified in placing so many bets on Crystal? It became a town in 1881, got a post office in 1884, and had over 500 residents soon thereafter. A not unpromising start, boosted again in 1906 by construction of the standard gauge Crystal River and San Juan line into the town of Marble to haul out marble slabs. The line also improved access for the Crystal mines. But the last train rolled in 1942, and the Crystal River and San Juan rails were torn up.

While lack of easy transport for years was the biggest handicap for the mines around Crystal, these mines never had the influx of capital and know-how like those in Aspen. Poorly financed Crystal miners typically worked their digs for one or two ores only, not recovering other values. Crystal never received attention from a first-rate engineering mind like that of Samuel I. Hallett. Hallett, a descendant of steamboat inventor Robert Fulton, developed and patented an effective process for recovering valuable secondary minerals (e. g. lead) from the silver ores of Aspen's Smuggler Mine. This process made the Smuggler mine reliably profitable. Such a mind, backed by sufficient capital, might have worked wonders in extracting more value from the complex Crystal ores.

Crystal is now just a shadow of its one-time bustling self. It is inhabited, not year round by rugged miners, but only in the summer by owners of second homes who like to "get away from it all." Porter Nelson's cabin still stands, adjoining the store serving the summer tourists who find the scenery and fishing attractive. Hardly what Nelson envisaged for the place where he invested so much of his time, so much of his scant money, and so many fragile hopes.

EPILOGUE

My major complaint about The Denver Post obituary for Porter Nelson is its brevity, but I have one more quibble. Was Porter Nelson really a "mining man?" I say no. True, he was a shareholder in, or officer of, several small companies operating mines. He did oversee the working of some of his own mines in Crystal for a time during the World War I mining boom. But most of his mining properties were bought with this aim: to sell them profitably when conditions improve. Rarely, I believe, did he buy a mine intending to conduct mining operations there himself. His business card from the good years in Aspen (see page 41) has it right in listing his business as "mines, mining stocks, bonds and other stocks." I think that he should be called a dealer in mining properties, as he was described in Denver city directories from 1929 on. Or called an investment or real estate adviser, as he was listed from 1917 to 1928.

Porter Nelson only briefly worked full time for others, e. g. the Santa Fe Railroad when he was getting started, and the N. H. Griffith Company when he was really down. In Aspen, he first worked on his own, buying and selling mining properties, and acting as Notary Public and trustee in property transfers. Later on, when he had less of his own capital to play with, he served as a "lone wolf" secretary for small companies with absentee owners: the Meadow Mountain Mining Company, the North Pole Mining Company, the Colorado Highland Marble Company, the Treasury Mountain Metals Company, the Grand View Mesa Irrigation Canal Company, etc. None of these companies was a great money maker, nor required his full time efforts. His work as a company secretary did not make him a "wage slave." Porter Nelson was more an "idea man," dreaming up enterprises like the

Aspen Home Mining Company, or the power plant on the Crystal River. Sadly, these typically went nowhere.

Politics was not a part of Nelson's life before Bryan's defeat in the 1896 election. Then Nelson must have felt that doing something to "save silver" was, for an Aspenite, akin to patriotism. No doubt that supporting the Peoples Party, dominant in Aspen and most vociferously pro-silver, seemed the clear choice for helping to bring silver back. As Peoples Party Mayor, Nelson showed greatest interest in improving the health, and morals, of Aspen. After his one term, he ran for no office (other than for the non-partisan School Board).

The Panic of 1907 seems to have been the straw that broke Porter Nelson's back. Many of his investments in silver and Aspen soured earlier, certainly by 1899 when he lost the "magic" silver dollar which guided his investment decisions. Still, the Nelsons seemed able to go on living the good life: a servant in the home, money easy enough for Porter to give each family member $10 in cash to invest. For a year from July, 1906, Julia Henry and the children were out of Aspen, either on vacation or for Julia Henry's health, in Colorado, in the East and then in California. In the spring of 1907, Nelson went on a multi-week, multi-man prospecting expedition in Nevada with James Stewart, an associate from the North Pole Mining Company. The expedition moved from Rhyolite, in Nye County in the south, to Buckskin in Humboldt County in the north, a range of some 300 miles. The expedition seems not to have found anything worthwhile, but it must have cost him plenty. By mid-1908, Porter Nelson's finances were clearly strained, and he never really recovered. Had he been depending on short term capital from October, 1907 to January, 1908 when overnight money rates in New York went to 75%? What else may have gone wrong?

EPILOGUE

Now, about Aspen. In the early 1890's, Aspen had proclaimed itself the world's greatest silver camp. After 1893, it never recovered its prominence. Its mines worked ores having a primary silver content, but with some lead. These ores became uneconomic at the low silver prices prevailing after 1893. Now, most of the silver produced in the United States is as a by-product of the mining of other metals. And it isn't just Aspen that has declined. Colorado, second only to Montana as a silver producer in the 1890's, now accounts for only 2% of US production. US silver output dropped after 1915, when the US was the world's largest producer with 40% of the world output, and an exporter. The US now is only in fourth place among world silver producers. No longer exporting silver, the US consumes twice what it produces.

The demise of silver arguably was needed to make Aspen a better place to live. Aspen now is not the bustling mining town Porter Nelson first knew, with ore processing plants belching noxious fumes, streams polluted with mill tailings (and manure), hillsides scarred with mine workings. Aspen Mountain now is smooth, grassy in summer and filled with skiers in winter. The city now is home, not for grubby miners but for "beautiful people" (and "beautiful prices").

By the 1870's, the fate of silver mining depended to a great degree on domestic politics (and to some extent on efforts to get international agreement on silver). In 1873, Silverites found allies who helped to push through the Coinage Act creating the heavy silver trade dollar designed for export. Allied with Silverites then were interests seeking an advantage in trade with the Orient. In 1890, the Silverites made a deal with eastern industrialists to push through the Sherman Silver Purchase Act. The industrialists supported the Sherman Act in return for Silverite support in raising a protective tariff.

Silverites also had farmers' support in the 1890's when farm prices were at record lows. When farm prices rebounded in the 20th century, farmers no longer made common cause with Silverites. During the Great Depression, the country was ready again to hoard silver, at tax-payer expense. This was not to help silver miners, but seen as a necessary step to overcome the economic crisis. From the 1930's Depression to the 1960's, the US Government held off the market a vast stock of silver bullion, amounting at times to over 2 billion ounces.

At present, the US Government holds only about 100 million ounces of silver. This is not to boost the silver price, but as a strategic reserve. Government reserves, even the large Depression reserve, did not do as much for silver as some Texas boys, aided by banks and Middle East speculators, did in 1980. Then the Hunt brothers of Texas tried to corner the market, holding contracts on about 300 million ounces. They were able to push the price of silver above $50 an ounce before their scheme collapsed. Old Aspen would love what the Hunts did, if only briefly, for the silver price.

The 16:1 ratio of silver-to-gold that the silver miners a century ago argued was their God-given right is far from the ratio set by markets today. Without anyone trying to corner either metal, the free market silver-to-gold ratio today is in the range of 75:1 to 80:1. Old Aspen would not enjoy seeing the value of silver so low in terms of gold.

After 1893, Silverites bemoaned the demise of "their" metal at the hands of the gold standard. The gold standard itself was brought down by the one-two punch of the Great Depression and the economic chaos caused by World War II. After World War II, only the US fully returned to the gold standard. Despite having accumulated most of the world's gold by the late 1940's, the US by the 1960's had to use "smoke and mirrors" to keep gold at $35 an ounce. When President Nixon in 1971 cut the last link between the US dollar and gold, he recognized the reality that the world valued one ounce of gold far more 35 US dollars.

The US Treasury still holds a large stock of gold at Fort Knox (although for what purpose is not clear). The International Monetary Fund still holds much of its reserves in real, not just "paper" gold (invented after World War II to supply liquidity without requiring more real gold to be mined). Both the US Treasury and the International Monetary Fund have sold off gold reserves in the past. They (and other national treasuries) probably will continue to sell gold into the private commodity market. Still, gold retains some of the aura of a monetary metal, something silver lost years ago.

I wish my grandfather could somehow be listening now, because I want tell him the following: "Granddad, our lives overlapped only for 23 years, and I was abroad for the last one of those. We met at most a couple of dozen times. We really did not get to know one another well. So I am glad that you learned to use a typewriter before most did, and kept copies of some of your correspondence (often frugally using the reverse side of papers that someone had sent you). I am glad that you preserved Julia Henry's letters from 1896, 1900 and 1909. These help me to understand you much better, now, than I did when you were still among the living.

"Better, yes, but there are still questions I wish I had asked you about certain events in your life. Example: what about your prospecting trip to Nevada in 1907? What was its origin? The photographs you left behind show more people involved than just you and James Stewart. Who else was there? Your expedition was in Nevada at a time when many exciting discoveries were made. Did your expedition find anything at all, or was it a total bust?

"A more important question: why did you chose to give up the good life you could have had in Virginia, and go to Colorado to work on the railroad? Was it primarily the adventure of it, escaping the staid life of Culpeper? Did you go to Colorado to escape a domineering father? Or was it fear of tuberculosis that impelled you move away? Your sister Kate died of tuberculosis in 1885; your younger brother George died early in 1886. You may have sensed that your brother Arthur, best man at your 1888 wedding, was also suffering from that disease. Did you think that in the dryer clime of Colorado, you would escape this Nelson tuberculosis curse? Or was your motivation the hope of making a fortune in Western mines, as people like Hearst, Walsh, and others were doing? Was it some combination of several of these?

"And why after the Panic of 1907 did you not do what your family wanted you to do, i. e. go back to Virginia where your well-off brother-in-law Clifford Miller was ready to help? I'd like to know the real reasons why you decided not to go back to 'ole Virginny.'

"A third big question: what role did Julia Henry play in your going to Aspen in 1888 and becoming a dealer in mining properties, a career for which your (and her) previous life was hardly adequate prelude? My grandmother Nelson died before I was born, so I never knew her. Was she a ready risk taker, too? And a related question: why, around 1900, were so many Nelson purchases of mining claim made in Julia Henry's name? Had she come into money of her own in 1895 when her step-father, James W. Carmer, died in Baltimore? Or in 1896, when the firm of which he was junior partner, Boykin, Carmer & Co., became Boykin & Stanley?

I realize that you had been burned by buying into Aspen and into silver just before gold mono-metallism vanquished silver. I can understand if you were therefore wary of silver, and of buying at the top. But did you, and she, seek to recoup by buying mining claims in past-their-prime gold areas where previous owners may have already taken a big beating? Was it her idea to confine such purchases to gold mining areas, like Cripple Creek and the Quartz Creek district of Gunnison County? Were these mining investments made in her name simply as insurance against seizure by your own creditors?

"My account of your life probably omits things of which you are proud, and justifiably proud. Such omissions are not intentional, but result from the inevitable dimming of the trail you left so many years ago. I realize that I have pointed out many unfortunate investments, and how your immediate family went through probably avoidable hardships because you elected to stay on in Colorado. Be assured that I really value the Colorado connection you and Julia Henry struggled to give me. Do not think that I set out with poison pen to write your story. Not at all; I wanted to describe your life honestly and frankly, fully expecting my account to redound to your benefit. In my eyes, the good of your life far outweighs any missteps on your part; I truly believe that I am not alone among your grandchildren in this feeling. My study of your life has deepened my admiration of your ability to dream, your ready optimism, your knack of persevering, with unflagging style, through setbacks that would have brought many to their knees. I cherish the passion for glittering ore samples (and small hydro-power installations), the love of mountain scenery and air, and the many other good things I owe to you. Thank you, indeed, W. Porter!

"Rest in peace."

INDEX

INDEX

CHRONOLOGY OF RELEVANT LAWS OF THE UNITED STATES

1792	Mint Act	(1 Stat. 246)
1834	Gold Coinage Act	(4 Stat. 699)
1834	Mint Act	(4 Stat. 774)
1837	Mint Act	(5 Stat. 136)
1872	Mining Act	(17 Stat. 91)
1873	Coinage Act (Trade Dollar)	(17 Stat. 424)
1875	Specie Payment Resumption Act	(18 Stat. 296)
1878	Bland-Allison Act	(20 Stat. 25)
1887	Trade Dollar Retirement Act	(24 Stat. 634)
1890	Dependent Pension Act	(26 Stat. 182)
1890	Sherman Silver Purchase Act	(26 Stat. 289)
1890	McKinley Tariff Act	(26 Stat. 567)
1900	Gold Standard Act	(31 Stat. 45)
1918	Pittman Silver Coinage Act	(40 Stat. 535)
1920	Mineral Lands Leasing Act	(41 Stat. 437)
1933	Economic Emergency Act	(48 Stat. 31)
1933	Silver Coinage Proclamation	(48 Stat. 1723)
1934	Gold Reserve Act of 1934	(48 Stat. 337)
1934	Gold Revaluation Proclamation	(48 Stat. 1730)
1934	Silver Purchase Act	(48 Stat. 1178)
1943	Suspension of Annual Assessment Work Act	(57 Stat. 74)
1943	Silver Use Act	(57 Stat. 520)
1946	Silver Industrial Use Act	(60 Stat. 750)